Near Breathing

Emerging Writers in Creative Nonfiction

Kathryn Rhett

near Breathing
a memoir of a difficult birth

EMERGING WRITERS IN
CREATIVE NONFICTION

This book is published by
Duquesne University Press
600 Forbes Avenue
Pittsburgh, PA 15282–0101

Copyright © 1997 by Duquesne University Press

Library of Congress Cataloging-in-Publication Data

Rhett, Kathryn, 1962–
    Near breathing: a memoir of a difficult birth / by Kathryn Rhett.
      p. cm.
    ISBN 0–8207–0277–3 (cloth: alk. paper).—ISBN 0–8207–0278–1
    (paper: alk. paper)
    1. Childbirth—Popular works.   2. Labor (obstetrics)—Case
    studies.   3. Delivery (Obstetrics)—Case studies.   4. Rhett,
    Kathryn, 1962– . I. Title.
RG652.R46 1997
362.1'985—dc21
[B]   96–51228
                                                        CIP

Several chapters, in slightly altered form, originally appeared in the following periodicals: Chapter 1 as "Labor and Delivery" in *Boulevard*; Chapter 2 as "Maternity" in *Creative Nonfiction*.

Lines from "All Hallows" from *The House on Marshland* by Louise Glück. Copyright © 1975 by Louise Glück. First published by The Ecco Press. Reprinted by permission.

In a few cases, to safeguard identities of persons or entities, name changes have been made in this work.

This book is printed on acid-free paper.

for Fred and Cade

And the wife leaning out the window
with her hand extended, as in payment,
and the seeds
distinct, gold, calling
Come here
Come here, little one
And the soul creeps out of the tree.

— Louise Glück

Contents

Acknowledgments

I feel enormous gratitude to the people who helped this account become a book. Jennifer Rudolph Walsh provided tremendous encouragement and assistance with revision. Lee Gutkind and Susan Wadsworth-Booth gave detailed analyses which led toward the final drafts; I am grateful for their commitment to the spirit of the book.

Early readers included Jane Angeles and Shane MacKay, who helped clarify the first chapters, explicated aspects of science, and urged me to keep going; and Pamela Mandell, whose comments about the beginning proved relevant to the whole. Other readers whose generous responses sustained me are Richard Burgin, Andrew Levy, Deb West, and Yoji Yamaguchi.

I'd like to thank my family, who faced the uncomfortable task of reading about themselves in occasionally less than flattering moments, and who allowed me to present my version of a story. Teel Oliver, Cecily Rhett, and Haskell Rhett offered insight and criticism throughout the writing process, asking fruitful questions.

Their belief in the worthiness of the project was crucial. Carol Leebron, Elizabeth Leebron, and Norman Leebron offered assistance with the facts, as well as unqualified support.

Finally, I thank Fred Leebron, who has contributed to this book in innumerable ways, from reading multiple drafts, to stretching our days to create writing time, to being my partner in love along this road.

Prologue

In the cemetery in our town, the catalpa beans lie scattered like burnt matches. Above, they hang greasy brown, in vertical clusters. The green beans we grew wait in a bowl at home. Cade has picked her first beans, and yesterday her first tomato. She steps onto the smaller gravestones and jumps off.

We climb to the highest point, over the crypts, to see Cape Cod Bay and the last arm of land flung around to form a harbor. The cemetery sprawls over irregular hills, set back from Commercial Street. We can see the white cupola bell-tower of Town Hall, where licenses are dispensed for outdoor restaurant seating and sidewalk vendors, where garbage disposal is debated, where the tourists can use a restroom, and charity events are held upstairs. The granite, Italianate Pilgrim's Monument towers over town. Cade used to call it the Monitor, and it does resemble a watchful being, with red lights in its top windows at night to warn airplanes away. The pilgrims stopped here to drink from a spring, then continued on to Plymouth. There are two cylindrical water towers, in a pale tablet-blue, and two brick buildings, the elementary school and the nursing home. Oak and pine surround the cemetery, making the town green, but in the distance, highest of all, is the creamy sand of a bare dune. On this peninsular strip, at the end of Cape Cod, water and sand will eventually run, and everything built will be gone. Is this why the pilgrims went on?

There are gravestones for children everywhere, many of the nineteenth century inscriptions still legible. We pick our way down the scrubby grass slope of a family crypt and I read the inscription above a clover-leaf opening in a stone door, for Annie, "who fell asleep June 4, 1882, aged 9 years, 8 months, 21 days." Nearby, Mary Louisa Bennett's stone reads, "We shall meet again. d. 1865 aged 11 months, 7 days." Here are five white marble stones, lined up like round-topped loaves of bread, on a slab which reads, "Children of Joseph P. and Delia C. Knowles." Of the worn inscriptions, I can make out a Millie, a Lizzie, and two who died in the years of their births, 1845 and 1855. The sun is hot today, wilting the dandelions, sparking crystals in the stones. Across the road, one family shares a polished granite marker. Frances Freeman, who lived to be 83, had a wife Mary J., who died, apparently in childbirth, in 1860 at age 38. The baby, Mary F., died too, in 1860, the number of days or months not noted. His second wife, Mary L., bore five children, two of whom died in the same year they were born. The other three lived until adulthood, dying between the ages of 31 and 42. Mary L. outlived Frances and all of her children. A carved fern decorates the top of the stone; to me it resembles a fossil print, a primitive, persistent form.

Now Cade is tired. She's had an ear infection and the medicine makes her stomach hurt. I pick her up. A white paper plate blows along high in the air, wheeling through this place, and out. Cade clasps her arms around my neck. I hold her tightly, feeling lucky. She is three. I expect so much.

1

I never imagined the perfect birth. I didn't script it, the way I did our wedding: when Fred and I decided to get married, I instantly saw myself in a white dress, surrounded by family, friends, and the neighbors from my childhood. "Why bring all these people together," my father said. "They won't get together again until someone dies." But he went along. My mother and I chose flowers for the tables, hors d'oeuvres to be passed on trays. It was an elaborate party, sprung whole out of my craving for normalcy, as a child of divorced parents and as a writer supported by part-time jobs. Someone said that before the ceremony Fred looked as if he might jump off the interior balcony into the ballroom, down into the ring of white-clothed tables. My sister and stepsister and I had to ride the hotel elevator eight times, stepping off at random floors to pace with our bouquets, before the entertainment manager would let us off at the mezzanine to proceed at the correct moment down the aisle. We were ready to throw up by then. Fred and I said the vows, ate the chicken, cut the cake, and danced to

Louis Armstrong's "What a Wonderful World," which we realized, as we boxstepped stiffly around, was about babies crying, and didn't sound romantic at all.

Two years later, though, I projected no image of childbirth, no picture comparable to the bride in white, until our baby was born, and I realized what I'd hoped for. The mother lies back, exhausted after her work, and receives the baby into her arms. They look at each other. What happens next? I wish I knew. There is an old Roman wedding vow which Fred and I would have spoken to each other if we'd known of it, and which we would have said to our child, a simple vow to set three travelers on one journey: *where you go, I go also.*

At the end of July, two days before my due date, we got ready for bed: I pulled on my white nightgown, and found a pillow to support my legs, even though I suspected the contractions were regular. I'd been having contractions for two months, since early June, and had spent four weeks in bed to forestall a premature birth. We lived in San Francisco then, in a fourth-floor apartment, and Fred moved our bed into a front room so I could enjoy the light through the bay windows. Jane had brought long stalks of gladioli and fanned them against the wall like a Mexican altar arrangement; Denise brought whatever bloomed in the garden she worked in, armloads of purple snapdragons or yellow roses. My mental life had left me—I didn't want to read books. I wanted to shop for the baby and organize the apartment; I'd already sorted our books by genre, and was about to separate the short story collections from the novels when I was sent to bed. I'd recorded contractions, and become accustomed to the hardening of the uterus under my skin. The skin across my belly was usually firm, but the baby's body could push against the uterine walls, making noticeable lumps. When the uterus contracted, it seemed unto itself, separate from me. I'd put my hands on the smooth hard rounded shape, and it was as if I held a ball, the baby suddenly unknown beyond the taut muscle. I wondered how the baby felt inside it.

This night, the contractions felt mildly painful, with a hint of potential hurting, a pinching at the cervix. We watched a rerun of "Cheers" on TV, at 11:30. "There's a contraction," I said to Fred, but without any urgency.

He was flossing his teeth. "Uh-huh," he said around the floss, having heard this at least a hundred times. We went to sleep. I slept between contractions, which were about twenty minutes apart. When I felt an adrenaline fear, I kept it down, telling myself, *Don't think of what's to come, be in the moment, stay focused.* I couldn't believe it was real labor. Everyone said first babies commonly came late. I breathed deeply through contractions. Fred slept beside me. Labor was unexpectedly peaceful so far, without blood or breaking waters or any sense of emergency. That a baby would emerge was still only an idea. I'd had an ultrasound at eight weeks and seen the gray fluttering heart, illumination beating against blackness, but it didn't look human; the heart looked like the gill of a fish pulsing, or a translucent fin swishing. When the baby grew, it became tangible but elusive—was that a foot or a hand, head or behind? It was a creature of weight, curves, and movement, mysterious knobs and jabs.

The sense of imminence made our time together fragile; never again would the three of us exist in this precise relationship. Fred and I enjoyed our nights at home, the sense of being cloistered before a great upheaval. Now we'd passed our last evening together as a husband and wife without a child. I was in labor. At 3:30 I woke Fred to say I thought this was it, and it hurt. I couldn't sleep anymore, but stayed in bed, resting and waiting for light. I told Fred to sleep, but woke him once in a while with quiet moaning. *Okay, okay, okay,* I'd say to myself, and run my fingers over my belly in circling patterns, a soothing movement called effleurage, which made me think of flowers. I was touching summer flowers, near-blooming zinnias, marigolds, orange lilies. At 5:30 the sky over Golden Gate Park looked like dark blue glass. When I was four, we'd lived for a year in London while my father wrote his philosophy dissertation, and the cobalt blue glass of English cathedrals had been imprinted on me: it was a soothing, revelatory color of first light. In the kitchen, I made tea and toast with jelly, and read *The New Yorker* at the black table. I tried very hard to concentrate on an article about coal miners in Siberia: there was a hovel with an earthen floor and a tin cup for water. There were the black mines, the blue-black coal dust. I was cold, drinking hot tea, reading about winter, the kitchen lit against the dark apartment. Secure in my lit chamber, and transported.

Then I took a shower and thought, *Next time I take a shower I'll have had a baby.* I dressed in cotton-knit old-man pants, pulled up high over the belly, and an enormous t-shirt. I combed my hair. Fred woke. We wanted to wait as long as possible before going to the hospital. In June, I'd spent two evenings in the labor and delivery area, lying on a narrow bed in a cold room with a monitoring belt around me. The bathroom was down the hall, in another labor room, where a woman moaned on a bed, tossing her head from side to side on the pillow. Her long dark hair and the dim room made the scene seem of another age, doom-tinged. I'd walked awkwardly back to bed, holding a urine sample in a paper cup with one hand, and trying to hold the gown closed over my bare behind with the other. Since so much of the fabric covered my belly, the hospital gown gapped widely in back. "This is a gown for a child," I'd complained to Fred. "Easy," he'd said back, as he stared at the ink lines forming huge waves on graph paper. "Your contractions are two minutes apart." Being at the hospital wouldn't help me relax.

It was more difficult to tolerate a contraction lying down, but sitting up tired me. Fred made the bed and retrieved the clock and the notepad I'd used to record early contractions. I watched TV. He edited a report that was due to the agency the next day; we'd been writing a series of reports commissioned by Levi Strauss about institutional racism in the communities where they manufactured. I wanted to help him, since he always wrote the first drafts, and then we alternated drafts, with me doing the final edit, or the "polish." For page eleven, though, I couldn't think of how to explain the way in which the Mexican sweatshop industry affected employment for Mexican Americans in El Paso, Texas. I pictured the nailed-together wooden shacks in Juarez, sewing machines humming in rhythmic runs day and night, but couldn't articulate the implications of this scene. "I can't abstract," I said. "Can't think."

"It's almost done," Fred said, writing quickly. "Don't worry."

I did the breathing tricks, the slow breaths, and the three slow breaths then a quick one. By 9:30 it was rougher. I lay on the bed and looked sidelong at Fred, who bent over a pile of papers on the table, making slashes with his pen. "Excuse me," I said, suddenly furious. "I'm in labor here."

He held his pen. "It's bad?"

"I'm lonely."

"I didn't realize. I'm sorry." The pen swooped. "Just a second." He flipped through papers. "Do you remember where the racial and ethnic school district stats are?"

I didn't answer. I looked at the floor and breathed. Fix your gaze on a spot, the childbirth teacher had said, and concentrate. When the contraction was over I said, "After the survey data. Stop working."

"What a mess." He threw down the pen.

"We're having a baby," I said. It seemed to me that he looked with great desire at the typed sheets strewn all over the table. "Fred."

He helped me sit up on the edge of the bed, and rubbed my back. Between contractions we finished packing the hospital bag—tiny baby clothes and blankets in a clean bag, lollipops, lotion, a paper bag for hyperventilation, bathrobe, slippers, and a new nightgown for after. By eleven o'clock the contractions were five minutes apart and almost regular. I breathed, panted, wandered from the kitchen to the bathroom to the bedroom, and sat on a straight-backed wooden chair. Fred moved the chair to the middle of the living room, because I wanted space around me. By noon I thought maybe we could wait longer to go to the hospital, but then I wouldn't be able to walk down the three flights of stairs and climb into a taxi. "Should I call?" Fred asked anxiously.

"I don't know." I sank into a musing about how much time it would take from the moment of the phone call to the moment of the taxi's arrival; and would we wait for the driver to ring the bell or watch for the car and then leave, or wait downstairs after we called; and did I need a coat?

"Wear the blue cardigan," Fred said, and breathed with me through a long contraction. "Should I call?"

"I really couldn't say." I was staring at an absurdly painted reindeer we'd bought in Mexico; little blue circles decorated its antlers, like Christmas balls hung on a tree.

He called. I walked down to the last landing and sat there, feeling huge and lost. I panted, saying, *Okay, okay. Keep that fear down.* I checked my watch—five minutes, yes, there's the contraction, five minutes, yes. Fred ran up and down the stairs checking the street and calling the taxi company again. Half an hour passed. The scenario of the pregnant woman who didn't get to the hospital in time was too familiar for a TV movie—my story would be relegated to a true-life series in which cheap actors re-enact the drama. A woman would be paid at an hourly rate to sit on the steps and pant like this. I laughed weakly. The taxi arrived.

When we pulled up to the emergency entrance, Fred paid the fare and asked for change, calculating a good tip for the driver—this was a significant taxi ride. We always tipped generously when we were about to get on an airplane, on the remote chance that unknowable forces were determining our fate. But Fred realized later that he had asked the driver for too much change, and the tip amounted to a miserly twenty cents. That miscalculation in a moment of being flustered, Fred later decided half seriously, must have turned luck against us, made a subtle alteration in the balance, so that everything that might have been all right instead turned toward misfortune.

In the hospital we walked down the long hall and I felt that people looked at me knowingly; I almost felt their hands on me and wanted to shake them off. On the fifth floor I signed in, and we waited in the seating area by the elevators. A man in blue overalls vacuumed. There were no magazines. There was the patch of carpet I'd passed out on when we took a tour of the labor and delivery department; I'd been hungry, and too long on my feet, and it was stifling in the narrow stalls of labor rooms 4, 5, and 6. I hadn't actually fainted, but had quickly guided my pregnant body in for a soft landing. I'd looked up at a teenager doing her home-work, a mother chasing a toddler; they were waiting for someone to have a baby. I'd thought, *My god, how will I survive labor, when I can't even make it through the tour?*

Fred touched my hand. "Are you all right?" What did that mean now? Could I manage not to faint in the waiting area? At least the carpet would be freshly vacuumed.

At 1:30, a nurse showed us to Labor Room 1, the biggest one, with a private bathroom. Securing the room was an unexpected coup, but now it seemed this was the only room I could survive in. A smaller space would have suffocated me. The nurse directed Fred to help me change into two gowns, one open in back and one open in front, like a nightgown and robe. What a clever system. I kept my socks on. I stood with my arms around his neck. The contractions hurt. The bag of helpful things, the washcloth, my old teddy bear, stayed packed in a corner. He helped me onto the bed so two nurses could strap on a thick brown elastic monitoring belt, with a clear gel under the metal parts for better transmission. The bed felt narrow, as if I could roll off.

They recorded contractions for twenty minutes and then removed the belt. I walked around the room. An obstetrician came in to check me. *Oh please be dilated,* I thought, as if it weren't my body, since somebody had to check it and tell me. Dilation was 3–4 centimeters at 1:45, 5 centimeters at 2:45. The baby was at station two, or two centimeters above the ischial spines; when the cervix was dilated to approximately ten centimeters, and the baby's head was at the level of the spines, it would be time for me to push. The doctor reached inside me and said, "I'm breaking your waters," as I felt the fluid running out. I wasn't sure why she did it, because the books I'd read didn't favor that. Later, we would read the medical records, which said, "Labor was remarkable for artificial rupture of membranes approximately five hours prior to delivery."

A new nurse came on at 3:00, and stayed with us in the labor room. Her thin hair kept working itself out of a low ponytail, and she pushed pieces of it off her face. She brought me a cup of ice chips. "You're doing well," she said. "Keep breathing like that." I was sitting up on the bed, my legs dangling over the side, rocking with pain and hanging my head down. I felt like a donkey, like silly Eeyore in the Winnie-the-Pooh books, who always looked glumly down; for an instant I felt like laughing, but then I felt beaten. I was swaying, my hair hanging down, and there was Fred's voice and him breathing, me breathing with him and keeping control of it. We didn't do the breath patterns, or signal with fingers like in childbirth class; we just tried to keep hold of it.

I stood up, and asked Fred or someone else for demerol, fentanyl, those words remembered from a notebook, from the hospital lecture on anesthesia in labor. Those preferred drugs had the least effect on the baby. "I need something," I said.

A doctor came in and explained the drugs would make the baby sleepy. I was thinking, they'll take the edge off, I just need the edge off, that's what they said demerol would do. And a contraction came, not just a burning, not ripping. More like a roar would feel, growing louder until you can't hear anymore. My uterus had taken over, so that I was nothing more than it was. The doctor said, "Do you understand what an epidural is?"

There was a pencil-point of light back there, a brain, thinking yes, and needles, complicated, numb, I don't need numb. The rest of me nodded stupidly. "Give me something," I said. And shut up, I thought.

"Oh, you've come so far," the nurse said. "Are you sure you need that?" I wanted to trust her, she'd been so nice. But 5 centimeters didn't seem far, when I had to get to 10. And the last centimeters supposedly hurt the most. That gripping. Was there time in between? Just when it seemed I would be conscious that I had survived a contraction, the next one would be upon me. They put an IV in my arm. I had to take in a certain amount of liquid before they'd give me the epidural. I felt tricked, as if they were deliberately delaying giving me relief. No one had said you had to wait for the liquid to drip in. With a kind of prayerful faith, I watched the clear liquid level falling. Let it fall, let it come in.

I was lying down, trying to breathe, watching Fred's mouth as he breathed with me.

An anesthesiologist came before 4:00. The nurse had set up a sterile instrument tray on one side of the bed and positioned me with my back to the equipment.

"I haven't used that before." The anesthesiologist pointed at the equipment.

The nurse seemed startled. "What should we do?"

"I use this one."

The nurse brought the tray around and helped me turn over. I had to lie on my side curled up and stay very still while the anesthesiologist put a needle in my spine. The image of a snail shell came to me, and one of those dark-brown striated worms you see curled up and dead. Fred held my hands. I whimpered when a contraction came. "Stay still," the anesthesiologist said.

Suddenly the pain stopped. It flowed away. I was released. I breathed, cautiously. I must have been on my side, but I felt as if I was on my back, loose-limbed and comfortable. I vaguely sensed a contraction, but it happened in some cavern of a uterus far away in my body, far removed from my head, my face, my shoulders, arms. I rested. The nurse wrote in her labor notes that I was feeling much more comfortable. They tested me for numbness by brushing cold alcohol swabs across my skin. I was numb to above my breasts. "Stations 5 and 6," someone said. They seemed concerned, and tested me again. According to the epidural anesthesia checklist, numbness should be confined to below station 4, the nipple line.

I may have slept, or lost consciousness. They kept taking my blood pressure, which felt like such an easy, uninvasive procedure. The blood pressure was dropping, to 72 over 40 by ten of five. I didn't care. If I ever have to die, let it be this way: in a sleepy and blissful state. Three doctors rushed in all at once. My blood pressure had been too low for over three minutes. An older male doctor (was he wearing a turban?) measured my blood pressure with an automatic cuff, then put ephedrine in the IV line. I was aware now, but not frightened, just watching. They had me lie on my left side, for better circulation, and put a clear oxygen mask over my nose and mouth. I hesitated to breathe for a second. I pictured oxygen masks dropping from the ceiling of an airplane cabin, dangling from yolk-yellow tubing, the clear bags remaining flat though oxygen was flowing through, or so they said. I inhaled. It felt like ordinary air.

Fetal heart decelerations were noted at 4:45, 4:50, and 4:55. An obstetrician wrote that the baby's heart rate always recovered. She anticipated a vaginal delivery soon. They did an internal exam and found I was completely dilated. The baby was at station zero, ready to descend into the birth canal. They attached a fetal scalp monitor. I imagined the metal square affixed to the head, a prick of blood. How anonymous the baby seemed then. Someone asked if they could turn off the epidural instead of just turning it down. "Yes," I said. It seemed funny they should ask. Since they'd told me not to have demerol or fentanyl, I'd felt entirely under their control. "Take a nap," someone said. Everyone except the nurse vanished into the outer room. I was supposed to rest until sensation returned and then start pushing. My cervix was completely dilated—nothing could hurt as much as it had before. I rested, feeling like the wan mother who's had the baby, pale with a pale half-smile. The fetal scalp monitor showed that the baby's heart rate occasionally dipped, and the nurse massaged my belly, saying that would help.

By a quarter of six, I felt something rear up inside me. I could feel everything, a hand on my skin. I could move my legs and feel them moving. I got up on my elbows and said I wanted to push. Fred and the nurse each held one of my legs. When I felt that intrusive pain, I pushed. Took a deep breath, held it in my throat, pushed. On some pushes the nurse would say, That's it, and on others, No. I couldn't tell the difference. Then I felt a subtle variation, a tilting down before the out, some slight directional movement I was making instead of trying to blast the thing straight out. She put a bar over the bed and I hung onto it and squatted and pushed. I had to take the oxygen mask off to talk and then let it snap back into place. The rubber seal around it felt hot on my skin. My legs got tired and I knelt. Then I stood on the floor, holding onto the bed. It felt lonely in the room, just Fred, the nurse, and me. Try this. Try that. I didn't think it would end.

When a contraction stopped, it let go completely, unlike earlier contractions. I could rest and breathe in between. It was hard to believe when another one came and I *had* to push this thing out. Everything got pushed out, little curls of shit, blood. The nurse kept cleaning me up. She filled in numbers on a vital signs chart; fetal heart decelerations occurred at 6:10, 6:45, 6:55, and 7:05. I felt split. The baby was surely too big. The childbirth teacher hadn't emphasized the unpleasant aspects of pushing— the tremendous pressure of the head as it enlarged the birth canal, the physical difficulty of pushing as hard as you could over and over. "Women feel empowered," she had said. "Instead of just passively surviving the pain, now you can do something about it." I cursed my preference for passively surviving pain. If only I had a different personality. It hurt. I couldn't. I shook, grunted, fell into high, keening whimpers after every push. The oxygen mask was hot. My voice was sharp and high, teetering off on a thread which ended raggedly in nothingness, in no control. Fred helped me down and then it would happen again.

"We see the head," the nurse said. "It's coming." She wheeled over a standing mirror. I saw a tiny oval of dark hair, smaller than an egg. I'd push and watch it enlarge and then sink back a little.

I'd lie on my side until the next contraction. Then I pushed, and it was so close, but not yet.

At 7:15 the nurse called in a doctor and another nurse. Dr. Greg, whom I hadn't seen before, put dark blue rectangles of sterile draping over my legs and across my pelvis. She fussed with instruments, asked for betadine, told me not to push. We had gone over this in class, yet I felt angry. I was being split and I could end this pain. The baby wanted to be born. I was aware of a quick long slash of an episiotomy. Anesthesia wasn't necessary; I'd wondered how a body could be in such a state that a knife cutting skin couldn't be felt. It felt as if she were drawing a line with her fingertip.

Labor had been nineteen hours. It was almost over. The doctor said, "Don't push yet." I tried not to, I held it for a second or two, and then I pushed the head out. The nurse exclaimed, "There it is!" I couldn't see anything beyond the blue draping. The pain was almost gone. I felt the wriggling, narrow body slip out as I pushed again. The pressure was gone. Everything happened behind blue cloths.

Dr. Greg asked, "What do I do now?"

The curly-haired jolly nurse who stood by my head said, "Put her up with mom." They laid the baby on my stomach. I could only see her from the waist up. Someone said, "Cute little fella." Her round eyes looked at me. She looked wise and silly, with wide-open blue eyes. I said hello. She blinked. This actual, particular person had arrived. She didn't make a sound. Then the jolly nurse lifted her up and took her out of the room, and Fred left, too. It was over. The baby was born. The terrific pain had ended, and my body began to wake up to lesser pains. I breathed through a light cramping. No one spoke. Dr. Greg stayed at the foot of the bed. After a few minutes, the nurse pressed on my belly. "Push now," she said. "The placenta is coming." I felt it sliding out of me.

A young bearded man in green scrubs came in, looking serious. He halted a few feet from the bed and crossed his arms. "They're working on your little girl," he said. "They're suctioning out the meconium." I nodded. Sometimes full-term babies had their first bowel movement, a thick tarry substance called meconium, before they were delivered; if they inhaled any of it, they had to be suctioned. This had happened to our friends' daughter, born that spring. The pediatricians had worked on her for a few minutes and cleaned her up, then given her back. "Okay," I said. I'd thought the baby was a boy, since someone had called her fella, and I lay there wondering at this. I'd fully imagined a boy and a girl, both alternatives, while I was pregnant, and it was odd to have the possibilities narrowed to one, then the other. Dr. Greg worked behind the blue drapes over my knees. The nurse put pitocin in my IV line, to help the uterus contract.

I could see the placenta in a pink plastic tub near my right foot, just the dark purple-redness of it. I didn't know, but my placenta was stained with meconium, indicating that the baby excreted meconium well before delivery, and so was probably in serious distress. They had to stitch me up. The red-haired doctor who I'd seen for preterm labor, Dr. Royce, came in. She told Dr. Greg what to do.

"Here's a trick I learned. You just loop that up."

"Oh really?" Dr. Greg said. "I usually loop it there."

I felt the needle pricking. "That hurts," I said.

"Like pressure?" the red-haired one said.

"I feel the needle." They looked at me as if they didn't believe me, shrugged, and injected me with a local anesthetic, which hurt. They went back to talking.

"Well, where I used to work . . ." Dr. Greg said.

"The way we do it here . . ." the red-haired doctor said.

Fred came in. He said the baby was having trouble breathing.

"She's a girl?"

He looked distracted. "You didn't know?"

"I couldn't tell. What's happening?" I wanted to know, and I wanted to talk. No one had mentioned how you had to lie on the bed getting stitched up for half an hour. What would happen next? The ends of the educational films we saw showed the baby being born and then handed to the mother wrapped in a blanket, everyone smiling.

"They're suctioning. I'll go see." He left. Dr. Greg and Dr. Royce stripped off their gloves and stood at the sink, washing their hands, then walked out. The nurse wrote notes on my chart. The draping still hung over my legs. The blue cloths were smeared with blood, as were the pink tub, the silver instruments on a table, the sheets of the labor bed, my gown, my hands. There was blood on my right hand and a brown stain on my left. The birth history, written by an intensive care nursery resident for July, describes the baby as having meconium-covered skin, and a pungent, sweet odor. I didn't remember touching her, but I had meconium on my hand. I stared at the stain.

The nurse removed the draping and covered me with a blanket. She was about to go on her dinner break, so she showed me how to massage my uterus, which felt like a hard tennis ball under the pouchy skin. A new nurse came in. She looked like a college student, bustling with energy, her permed brown hair in a high ponytail. "Let's get you into some fresh gowns," she said. "And maybe I can find you dinner." I was hungry, and bloody, and didn't think I could move.

Fred came in. They would be bringing the baby back to the labor room in a few minutes. I asked him to call our parents. He hesitated. But the baby was fine, wasn't she? Then why not call? He left to find a phone. The nurse gave me a damp cloth and I wiped my hands clean. At 8:30, she brought dinner on a tray.

There were two containers of juice, and I put one aside for Fred. The IV for fluids was still in my right hand. Holding the fork awkwardly in my left hand, I ate everything, the weird soft meatloaf, potato slices, roll, cut beans, cookies and milk, and thought of nothing else but eating, how good it was to eat.

Then I had to go to the bathroom. The nurse helped me sit up and swing my legs over the bed. She helped me stand and take small, slow steps to the bathroom, pulling the IV cart along with one hand and supporting me with the other. I felt dizzy and stopped, then went on. She gave me a bulky sanitary pad and a belt contraption, made of white elastic with gray metal hooks. White light bounced off of the white-tiled walls of the bathroom. I had to pee, but I couldn't. Fuzzy clumps of bright blood floated in the toilet. I put on the pad and belt and washed my hands at the sink and made my way back to the bed and lay down. The nurse fixed me a surgical glove filled with crushed ice to put on the episiotomy site, held in place with the pad and belt.

Fred came back. He stood by the bed and held my left hand. "She's in intensive care."

"I thought she was fine," I said. "They were going to bring her in."

"They were." He stroked my hand gently. "She's still having trouble breathing."

"Did you talk to anyone?"

"A doctor. They're working on her, so he didn't say much."

A hard bead of fear was growing in my chest; I willed it away. "I saved you some juice," I said.

"We can go see her."

The nurse said I'd have to pee or be catheterized before I could leave the room. I didn't want to be catheterized. Every few minutes, I shuffled over to the bathroom to try again, dragging the IV cart. I was bleeding and bleeding, and kept changing the pad, hooking a new one onto the barbaric belt. Women used to have to wear these all the time, I thought, and what did they use before the belt was invented? Rags, I thought, rags, thinking of anything to keep from thinking. Fred helped me get dressed in underwear, two new gowns, socks and slippers. I stood at the sink and washed my face.

The bearded man in scrubs came back in, and cleared his throat. I turned. "I want you folks to know that we're doing all we can," he said. "But it's touch and go." Neither of us said anything. We stood still in front of the sink. The man blew out his breath and stared at his sterile-slippered feet.

"Thank you," Fred said. The man left.

Fred put his arm around my waist. "Are you okay?" he whispered.

"I'm cold."

He helped me put on my robe. I tried to keep that neutral feeling I'd been practicing for the past 23 hours, of keeping the fear down and focusing on the present. In the low light, it was difficult to see my reflection in the mirror, but I carefully brushed my hair.

Fred shuttled between the intensive care nursery and the labor room, checking on the baby, checking on me. The ICN notes describe the baby upon admission as pale, with poor eye contact and coarse, raspy breathing. The heart rate was regular, but with a murmur. Manual ventilation failed to stop her respiratory distress, so she was put on a mechanical ventilator that pumped pure oxygen through a tube in her trachea into her lungs. The resident recorded her mental status as "stunned" and "spacey." By nine p.m., an arterial catheter had been installed in her umbilicus so that blood could be drawn quickly and painlessly; blood was immediately sent to the lab for a complete blood count and measure of oxygen content. IVs for antibiotics and morphine were started. At 9:10, a radiologist wheeled a portable X-ray machine into the nursery and took pictures of her chest and abdomen to check the placement of the endotracheal tube and umbilical catheter, and to evaluate her lungs. The X-ray showed fluid in the lungs. The left lung appeared completely white, or obstructed, with meconium, and the right lung showed patches of white. After seeing the X-ray, the resident pulled out the breathing tube one centimeter, since the tip had been pressing on the ridged tissue at the top of the baby's lung.

Dr. Hanover, the staff neonatologist, arrived in the ICN by 9:30. The baby was quiet, and responded to his examination by opening her eyes. Her eyes wouldn't focus. He described her as a full-term AGA, or average-for-gestational-age infant, and diagnosed meconium aspiration and pneumonitis. He wrote out directions for IV fluids, including albumin to increase her blood volume, since her pressure was low. He wrote out a series of if-then equations for ventilator support: if her blood oxygen is x, do y.

But I didn't know any of this yet. I'd been waiting for my baby, my baby daughter, for some time. I'd eaten dinner, and gotten dressed in clean gowns, and brushed my hair. She'd been taken away, and surely they'd had enough time to clean her up. I couldn't picture what they might be doing. I wouldn't even try.

Two hours had passed since her birth—wasn't that quite a lot of time? Of course, labor was nineteen hours, two hours wasn't so long. But it couldn't be normal for a baby to be taken away for that long, could it? The nurse said nothing, except to ask if I needed an icepack, or more water. The man said "touch and go," which meant she might not live. They weren't bringing her back, Fred had told me, and I finally understood it to be true: no nurse would walk through the door carrying my baby, wrapped securely in a white flannel blanket, and lower her into my arms. I stared fixedly at the oversized beige door and realized that I wasn't waiting for my baby anymore, but only for news of her.

2

Only the short fluorescent bar over the sink was lit; most of the delivery room fell into brown shadows. The placenta in its pink tub had been carried away. The sterile instruments were gone, as well as the deep-blue cloths. My bed projected into the room like a high, narrow bier. I was supposed to be resting. I felt tranquilized, or stunned. I didn't picture anything—what the baby looked like or where she might be, or even Fred walking down the hall toward me, though I was waiting in this blank place for him to return. I did not think, *If the baby has a problem I will feel x, if the baby is fine I will feel y.* I could not imagine what was taking so long for Fred to come back, or anyone to bring me news, and I did not try to imagine. The nurse had cleaned up the room nicely, gathering bundles of bloody cloths, directing an orderly to mop the circles of blood on the floor. She'd placed a cup of ice water next to the bed. Now she sat in a low armchair, going through papers, making a note here and there. I closed my eyes. A wide fan of light opened them—Fred was back. He held my hand. "She's on a respirator," he said.

I struggled to sit up halfway. "It's breathing for her."

"Yes."

"The doctor said?"

"He said we have to wait and see."

The room—with its beige walls, reflective beige linoleum tiles, vinyl-upholstered chairs, steel sink—felt sealed, too neutral. A good thing could happen here, or a bad thing. The room didn't care, the room wouldn't show a trace of it. I wanted out.

The blankness I'd kept so willfully had narrowed into a narrative line: first the baby was carried away by a nurse to be suctioned and cleaned up, then she wasn't brought back to me, and now a machine breathed for her. Where was the line going? What would the history be? Once I was in a train accident, a derailment outside of Philadelphia, and what happened wasn't the worst—the car turned on its side and was dragged along the tracks. The sensation of hurtling without limit had scared me most. "Maybe we should call my mother," I said. She headed the Washington, D.C. office of a pharmaceutical company. "She could call someone for advice."

"Right," Fred said, then whispered, "It's not as if Bismarck Hospital has a good reputation."

"Exactly." People around the neighborhood and in my exercise class had often asked where I'd be having the baby. Children's Hospital, or UCSF? When I answered Bismarck, they sometimes said, Good luck, as if I'd need it. We'd switched to a cheaper insurance plan in my second trimester, as soon as we were eligible through one of Fred's employers, to the HMO hospital Bismarck. All of my pregnancy and delivery costs would be covered, and the hospital, while not as plush or prestigious as UCSF, seemed just fine. I'd signed on with a highly recommended obstetrician, who didn't happen to be on duty that day.

When Fred left, I went into the bathroom yet again and

commanded myself to pee, and finally I did. I would be released into the outside light soon.

"How much do you think you did?" the nurse asked.

I wondered how much I was supposed to do, and how you could calculate such a thing. A quarter cup, I told her, which was an acceptable amount—she disconnected my IV line.

She called in the delivery nurse, who came in with Dr. Greg. They picked up a clipboard holding birth information and a post-partum recovery checklist. Vital signs were stable, bleeding was normal, and voiding had been accomplished. The delivery nurse, plump, with short curly hair and round-framed glasses, resembled a child's stuffed owl. She'd spoken to our childbirth class for an hour about the process of labor. We must have looked nervous, listening closely, our chairs arranged in a perfect U. So serious, she'd teased us: You'll all survive. Now she ignored me.

"You sign off here," she said to Dr. Greg, raising the clipboard up high. Dr. Greg held her body tall. Her straightened hair was styled in a smooth cap, her dark-brown skin gleamed. She hadn't spoken to me, except to say, Don't push yet. She tilted down and signed. I rested on the bed, watching them. They talked to each other as they left the room. *Why didn't they speak to me*, I wondered. Did they know how my baby was doing?

The delivery nurse came back in with a wheelchair, smiling, and said she would take me to see the baby. I said, "My husband's on the phone. He'll be right back."

She said, cheerfully, "Oh, let's go now." She helped me in and put a blanket over my legs. The skin of my arms was mottled pink with cold; I'd always disliked the transparency of my skin. Did we have to go now because the baby might not survive another five minutes? She pushed me into the hall. The rubber wheels on linoleum made a seamless whispering sound. The hall was empty. It was after ten o'clock at night; the baby had been born two and a half hours before. We turned a corner and there were windows into a room on my right. She pushed me through a doorway into a reception area outside the intensive care nursery. I sat up straighter in the chair. "There's your baby," she said and pointed to a group of people in front of a high table.

Fred appeared beside me. "There she is," he said, and held my hand. He'd already been here. She lay on her back, with her limbs splayed and a thick plastic tube rising out of her mouth and curving away to a machine. She was hard to see, because the table was high, and on the other side of a window, and people dressed in blue scrubs clustered around adjusting machinery that flanked her table. Bright light shone down on her, on her body laid out flat, punctured with tubes. I couldn't see what her face looked like, or her hair.

The supervising nurse sat on a stool in the nursery, writing notes. Our names were Fred and Kathryn; we were married, and English was our primary language. There had been no complications of pregnancy; the baby was delivered vaginally, with a delivery complication of meconium. The baby had grunted and flared her nostrils in an effort to breathe. Her body had been pink but her face was still blue when she arrived in the ICN. The baby could move all of her limbs, and was active, with a weak cry. Her immediate equipment needs were a ventilator and a warming bed.

"You can't go in right now, her settings are still being adjusted," the unit assistant told us. His blowdried yellow hair gave off a lacquered shine. He held a black telephone receiver with his shoulder. "Come back in a few, you can sit with her," he said, then talked into the telephone. The anteroom was crowded with equipment, trash barrels, a scrub sink, a water dispenser; there was hardly room for the wheelchair. I felt I would cry. I turned to Fred at my side and said, "Let's go now." Then I looked down at my lap so as not to see any more. He wheeled me backwards out, and down the hall.

We passed through the open central area of labor and delivery, where nurses watch the bank of monitors, and returned to the labor room to collect our things. A nurse led us to a maternity room, at the end of a hallway, and directed us to a bed at the right of the door. There was a box of surgical gloves for perineal icepacks, and Fred went to fill a new glove with ice. To the left of the door, a dark-haired woman slept in a bed. Next to it, a tiny baby wearing a knit cap slept in a clear plastic bassinet on wheels. There was an empty bed at the back of the room.

Fred brought me the glove, lumpy with ice. We whispered. He pulled the white curtain that hung from a track in the ceiling and moved my visitor's chair to the foot of the bed so I could get to the bathroom more easily. He hung up my robe, put my hairbrush on the shelf, and filled the water pitcher. I asked for my ragged old bear, and hid it under the bedsheet. In the bathroom, as instructed, I sprayed myself with the squirt bottle, then used a towelette instead of toilet paper. I ran it lightly over the stitches, feeling a large swollen ridge. There was so much blood in the toilet. I unhooked the bloody pad, threw it away, and attached a fresh one. The elastic of the belt was soaked with blood near the hooks. Underwear helped hold the pad in place. I took a few careful steps out into the room to the bed, picked up the ice glove, and eased it into place. I walked to the wheelchair outside the door and sat down, with my weight on one side so as not to sit directly on the icepack. Fred put a blanket over my legs.

We rolled down the corridor, past the shut door of Labor Room 1, around a corner. I felt awake, and more in control after having arranged my belongings in the room. The intensive care nursery wouldn't be a shock the second time. From the anteroom

I could see her, alone now, on the high table. We washed our hands at the scrub sink, for the required five minutes for first-time visitors, then put on puffy yellow paper gowns. Fred wheeled me in. A pink card taped to the wall had "Baby Girl Rhett" written on it. She was almost four hours old. Light shone on her from two warming lamps mounted above the bed. She lay on her back, eyes closed, with a tube coming out of her mouth, strips of clear tape on her upper lip holding it in place. Her nose was unobscured by tape—it was so perfectly modeled, whole and unharmed. Dark brown hair matted against her head. A skinny tube curled out of her bellybutton. An IV was taped onto her right hand. An un-fastened disposable diaper lay under her. Her left foot was wound with gauze, which held a round red light in place. The table was at chin level for me in the wheelchair, and had six-inch-high clear plastic barriers around the sides. I leaned closer. A man's voice behind me said, "You can touch her."

It was Dr. Hanover, stout, red-faced, white-bearded, in scrubs, who leaned against a sink and watched the baby. We introduced ourselves. He didn't say much, but seemed friendly enough, though his big hammy arms stayed crossed on his chest. He explained that the baby had aspirated meconium deep into her lungs, and that her lungs had stopped working. The respirator breathed for her. She was being given a glucose solution through one IV for nourishment, and antibiotics through another to pre-vent infection.

"Meconium is nasty stuff," he said. We nodded silently. She looked exposed, with no diaper or t-shirt on, no cap or socks, no blanket. We all watched her, her chest moving up and down rapidly. He told us she'd probably need a blood transfusion. "We're giving her morphine, too."

Was there a limit to this? I turned halfway around in the chair. "Could she die?"

With his arms still crossed, he shrugged his shoulders. "Yes," he said. He drew out the word as if to qualify it. "We have to wait and see." He left the room.

The nurse gave us an information packet about the ICN. She went back to her clipboard, where she filled in our names on a checklist about impaired parent-infant attachment due to hospitalization. Parents should demonstrate a parent-infant attachment by: holding/touching infant, calling infant by name, and making eye contact with infant. On a separate sheet, under the heading of Parent Contact, she wrote that both parents appeared calm at this time, but seemed to understand the situation. We had talked to the baby and held her hand. We'd both stated that we understood the baby's present condition. Under the heading of Nurse's Notes, she continued her detailed description of the baby's status and treatment, how what they were suctioning from her breathing tube at regular intervals was turning from meconium to bloody secretions, from hemorrhage of the lungs.

We had to leave for change of shift, when one nurse would go off duty and another would come on for the overnight hours. "Please rest," I said to the baby. "We'll be back to see you soon." She could know my voice, and might be soothed by a neutral tone. I touched her wrist with a fingertip.

"Goodnight honey," Fred said. He swiveled my wheelchair around, and pushed me out. We took off our yellow gowns and crumpled them into the trash container.

"What do you think?" I said to Fred.

He sighed. "You need to sleep."

There were two parents' rooms opposite the nursery, but both were occupied. Fathers were not permitted to sleep in the maternity rooms, so Fred would sleep in a waiting room near the ice machine. He wheeled me down the dark hall to my room. I felt overwhelmed by tiredness and pain. Whereas earlier I'd chosen not to think ahead, now I was unable to think of the future, of what her machines and tubes and needles foreboded. I would sleep first, think later.

"I'm sorry to wake you," a voice said, "but I've got to take your vitals." It was midnight. An obstetrician put a thermometer in my mouth and took my blood pressure. She turned down the covers, put her hand under my gown, and pressed her open hand on my abdomen. "Feels good. Are you massaging that?"

"Some," I said, which was a lie, since I'd practically forgotten about my uterus. She checked my bleeding, which was normal. She said someone would come in a while to show me how to use the breastpump. I wondered how long a while would be, and if I had to wait in the room so as not to miss this breastpump person. It occurred to me that nights were like days to the night shift staff, with scheduled appointments for 2:30 a.m., 4:15.

At 12:30, a nurse took my blood pressure and asked how I was feeling.

"Sore. I think I need more ice." She left and returned with a fresh ice-glove. The ice-gloves worked, though they seemed primitive. I tried for a few seconds to arrange the rubber ice-fingers so they touched my stitches. God, if I could just move the thumb off my thigh, I thought in frustration, and almost burst out laughing.

The nurse was serious. "Your baby is in the ICN?" she asked softly.

"Yes," I said. She went back to her desk in the hall. She wrote, "Encouraged patient to express her feelings," an action required by the nursing protocol, in the case of an ill infant. "Patient stated baby was in the ICN," she wrote.

Fred appeared at the door. "Can't sleep?" he whispered, almost hopefully.

"I can't." He helped me out of bed.

We were hungry. The maternity ward slept. A few nurses made notes on pads at their desks in the hall. Their reading lamps lit only the surfaces of the desks, and glinted off one nurse's eyeglasses. We went through double doors and turned left to the elevators. Two floors up, there were vending machines for juice, coffee, candy bars and gum. A machine with revolving shelves offered yogurt, pastries, sandwiches.

"How much money do we have?" I asked.

"Get whatever you want."

I said, "I don't know what I want. What do you want?"

"I want a burrito." He pushed coins into the machine. "And a raspberry seltzer."

"That's not really seltzer, it's full of sugar. You don't want that."

"I want it. What do you want?"

"I want a cinnamon roll and an orange juice."

In the adjacent snack bar the chairs were up on tables, and a janitor's bucket and mop stood on the floor. We took our drinks and straws, napkins and food in crackling plastic back downstairs, to Fred's waiting room. He turned on the lights and shut the door. We sat underneath a television set that winged out from the wall like an enormous dental instrument. We ate with solemn concentration. We asked, "Are you all right?" to each other and said "Yes."

"Piece of cake," Fred said, with a short laugh.

"No problem," I said. "I'm so glad we took that childbirth preparation class." Then we started laughing and couldn't stop. I laughed hunched over in the wheelchair, tilted sideways and holding my stomach, and Fred laughed with his head thrown back, wiping lettuce shreds from his mouth. The carpeted walls seemed to absorb and deepen the sound.

"Nearly dead baby," Fred sputtered. "They ought to do a film on that."

"With a respirator scene—we had no idea what to expect."
We were gasping.

"Shush," I said finally. "I have to pee." Fred was sitting soberly
on the couch when I came out. "It'll be okay," I said, touching his
shoulder.

He stood up and hugged me. We stayed like that for a while.
Two years before, we'd made a plan that seemed improbably
long-term for us, to travel for a year and then return to the United
States and have a baby. When we moved back to San Francisco,
Fred wasn't sure that he was ready, considering our uncertain
financial prospects. If only my body were eternally young, I said to
him, I'd prefer to wait, too. We could try to publish books first,
work as tenure-track teachers instead of adjuncts, and own a
house. We could travel more, stay up late more, and write as
much as we wanted. We'd created an enjoyable pattern in the
seven years we'd been together, of working many hours at five
different jobs for a year or so, and then getting on a plane and
escaping. We'd been through two master's programs together, a
postgraduate fellowship for me, a year at Stanford for him. We'd
spent two summers in Portugal and a year traveling. I liked reading books at two in the morning as much as Fred did; I wanted to
live in India and Brazil, too. I hated the term "biological clock,"
and hated that the cliché had come true for us: me persuading
Fred that we should have a baby while he came up with reasons
for stalling. After we'd been home for a few months, we could
afford health insurance that covered pregnancy, and Fred agreed
to start trying. We both thought we'd have time to become accustomed to the idea, seven or eight months at least, but within a
month I was pregnant. Sometimes we expressed ambivalence
about having a baby, until a friend asked cautiously, Was it a
planned pregnancy? Yes, it was, but we were anxious about the
profound change in our lives. It amazes me: we were worried

about the consequences of having a healthy baby.

Fred wheeled me to my room, and returned to his waiting room. I woke to light and voices at 2:30. "The baby was soaked," an unfamiliar nurse scolded the woman in the other bed. "You've got to get up and change him." The curtain between us was partly drawn. The mother was half-sitting up, and a nurse held the baby. The mother protested in a soft, foreign-accented voice, maybe Middle Eastern. Her long hair was falling out of its bun. She sounded exhausted. "Well, he was wet through," the nurse declared. "And now he's hungry." The baby squalled, though not loudly. The nurse thrust him at the mother, and returned to her post outside the door.

I didn't want to ask the crabby nurse for more ice. I got out of bed carefully, without sitting up, and put on my slippers. I shuffled in short sliding steps down the hall. It wasn't too difficult. I could walk, wasn't dizzy. At the tall aluminum machine, I filled a glass with crushed ice, then crossed the hall to use the sink and counter space, where I dumped ice in the glove, working some into each finger. I twisted the open end and wrestled it around my finger to tie it like a balloon. I felt competent, myself again. I eased open the waiting room door. Fred slept curled up on his side on the couch, his arms crossed. We'd brought a blanket his grandmother knit to the hospital and this lay over him. I pulled it up to his shoulders. I didn't want to wake him. I closed the door behind me and shuffled back to my room. The woman slept. Her baby slept again in his bassinet. I slept, comfortably, according to the nurse.

At 3:30 I woke up and got out of bed. Fred came through the door as I was putting on slippers. "You're awake," he said. He helped me into the wheelchair in the hall and we went quietly down corridors and around corners.

As we passed Labor and Delivery, I whispered, "We should name her."

Fred stopped the chair. "So soon?"

"What if she died without a name? It would be cruel." Her spirit could pass from us, unclaimed, I thought. Unloved.

Fred stood in front of me, staring off to the side. "Maybe we should wait."

"Until?"

"Until we know."

"No." We were immobilized in the hallway. He thought naming her would finish her, close her like a box. The gravestones of infants had names. "We need to welcome her," I insisted. "Call her to us. She's our child."

"Will it be Cade then?" he said tiredly.

I conceded him that. He got behind the wheelchair and pushed. I wished for Lucy, or Jane, but Fred didn't like those names. We'd recently agreed on Cade, my maternal grandfather's middle name, with Emery, my father's and my middle name. His family would be represented by the last name, and both sides of my divorced family by the first and middle names. But what about a name for her? Did I think she wouldn't live, so I might as well placate everyone?

We arrived at the brightly lit anteroom of the ICN. Fred pushed me up to the sink, and we scrubbed and gowned. The nursery was dark except for reading lights, monitors, and the baby's warming lamps. She lay on her back, her head turned to the left. The nurse stood, smoothing down tape around an IV on the baby's hand.

"How is she?" Fred asked.

"She's hanging in there. You all should get some rest."

"Can't sleep," I said.

"It's hard." She retreated to her chair.

We each put a finger on the baby's right hand, avoiding the taped-down needle. Fred whispered, "We name you Cade Emery

Leebron," and I repeated it. "We love you," he said. How did we love her, I wondered. My emotions were suppressed, as if I weren't breathing. The baby was hardly breathing, the baby couldn't cry with the ventilator tube in her mouth.

A young woman in blue scrubs approached and ran her fingers through her short hair. She'd been working for twenty hours. "She's breathing more easily now than a few hours ago, so that's good. We're trying to stabilize her, and it looks as if she's heading in the right direction."

"Good," I said.

"It's difficult to say right now," the resident said quickly, as if anxious not to mislead us. Her expression fell into a bland smile. She was short and stocky, with a wide face, unwrinkled skin.

"Of course," Fred said. "We understand."

"Dr. Hanover explained we would have to wait and see," I said.

"That's right." She looked relieved. "I was just going to check her breathing tube." She stood still at the head of the bed.

"Oh," I said, after a few moments. "Should we go?"

The nurse wrinkled her nose. "It's best. Did you get an orientation packet?"

"Earlier, we did," Fred said. We hadn't read it yet.

"Usually when a procedure is performed, we ask that the parents leave," the nurse said.

Fred leaned over the bed and whispered, "We'll see you in a little while, sweetie." He touched her forearm.

"Mom and Dad love you," I said. I reached over the barrier to touch her, too. He wheeled me out.

My blood pressure was taken at 4:30, and then I slept until six o'clock, at which time the nurse noted that I was ambulatory in the hallway, walking with difficulty. I met the lactation specialist wheeling a contraption toward me, and followed her back into the room. She stood next to a square metal box screwed onto a cabinet with wheels, the kind of functional blondwood cabinet you might see in an elementary school classroom. She suggested I sit in bed. She tore the paper cover off of a plastic box and began handing me things: clear rubber tubing, a funnel, a cup. The wide end of the funnel fit over my breast. I should pump for a few minutes on each breast to start, every hour or so, the nurse said, to encourage my milk to come in. By the afternoon, I should be pumping for fifteen minutes on each breast every three hours. Watching TV might help me to relax. The nurse left. I fell asleep until 7:30.

The stitches hurt. A nurse's assistant brought me an ice-glove. I used the clicker near my pillow to raise the back of the bed. I could sit with my weight on one side. By leaning far to the left, I could just reach the breastpump cabinet and maneuver it close to the bed. I attached the tubing to the pump and turned it on. Rroom, rroom, rroom, it ground out in rhythmic efforts. Hesitantly, frowning, I brought the funnel to my breast. Rroom, rroom, rroom—the nipple got pulled out toward the narrow bottom of the funnel. It didn't feel so bad. I checked my watch to time five minutes. Maybe it hurt a little. I turned the dial back to minimum. A few yellow drops emerged and meandered unimpressively into the collection cup.

Breakfast arrived in an airline-style cart. The clatter of plastic trays woke the baby in his bassinet, and he cried a baby-cat cry behind the half-drawn curtain. His mother painfully eased her way out of bed. She looked over at me. "Cesarean," she said. "The stitches." She lifted her baby from the bassinet and held him against her shoulder. The orderly pulled the breakfast cart backwards out of the room, and then the doorway was full of people: another mother, a nurse, a tightly swaddled baby sleeping in a bassinet, and a husband. The nurse helped the woman into the bed at the back of the room. She pulled a long curtain across, blocking my view. I would have to pass through a corner of her area to get to the bathroom. I ate the sticky bun, cereal with milk, scrambled eggs and toast. I drank juice. It was lonely to be in this room without Fred. As if I'd been packed off to a strange overnight camp, I wanted to be sporting—eat the food, act cheerful, follow the schedule—but I really wasn't in the mood to be a good patient, a nice patient, a patient at all. The mother next to me watched TV, with the volume on high. The newest mother's husband talked excitedly into the telephone, in an unfamiliar language. I wanted to go home.

We visited Cade in the nursery, becoming marginally aware of the system of protocol, technology, and personnel that we were now a part of. We got used to washing our hands at the large white scrub sink with red liquid soap, and fastening the yellow paper gowns. I put my hair back in a ponytail before I went in. We sat by the side of her table-bed, me in a wheelchair and Fred on a stool. Dr. Hanover had told us to touch her and speak to her because she recognized us, and knew that we weren't there to hurt her. Everyone else who touched her moved her breathing tube, or inserted needles. Fred reached over the plastic barrier and touched her arm. "Hi, Cade," he said. "Your mom and dad are here."

"We're here with you, sweetie," I said, smoothing her hair, which had dried in stiff points. A machine beeped, rapid high-pitched tones, and we both started and pulled our hands away. What had we done?

The nurse jumped up from her stool, looked at the baby, and hit a black button on a monitor hung near the foot of the bed. We stared at the black monitor screen, two sets of red glowing numbers. "What happened?" I said.

"Her blood pressure dropped," the nurse said.

"Because we were touching her?"

"It would probably be best if you didn't disturb her now." We kept our hands in our laps. The blood pressure climbed. From then on, we restrained ourselves and gently touched her hand with our fingertips and whispered when we arrived and left. Surely we could at least let her know we were there.

The machines were bewildering at first. I thought about my sister-in-law Betsy, whose second son had been born early and put on a respirator. I would have to learn these machines and ask questions and be my baby's advocate, as she had been for Jonathan. The respirator near the head of the baby's table showed how many breaths per minute she was being given and the percentage of pure oxygen she was getting: 90 percent, as opposed to the air we breathe, which is 20 percent oxygen. Two square sensors on the baby's chest sprouted wires that ran to the heart rate and blood pressure monitor. Halfway down the bed, there was an IV cart with a bag of clear glucose solution hanging from it, a bag of golden liquid antibiotics, and a flat box with a digital readout of how much had been given.

The doctors, nurses, and respiratory therapists all introduced themselves to us and encouraged us to come back when we left. We were aware of being in the way, though, our chairs blocking the narrow space between Cade's bed and the sink; everyone had to pass through this space to get into the room. People squeezed past us to attend to the other baby in this room of the nursery, or to get to Cade, to wash their hands, to use the telephone, or to get supplies from a large wall cabinet. We came and went, donning and discarding yellow paper gowns. I doubt I'll ever choose to wear that color again in my life, ICN yellow. It was Wednesday morning. Cade had been born twelve hours before, on Tuesday night.

We met with the neonatologist on duty that day. He brought us into the office across the hall from the nursery, sat us down, and explained meconium aspiration and persistent fetal circulation. He quickly sketched the lungs, with blood vessels, on a pad, and explained that as blood passes through the vessels of the lungs, it is oxygenated. When our baby inhaled meconium, it went deep into her lungs and caused an immediate system shutdown. Her blood vessels clamped shut, and they still hadn't relaxed open. As a result of the clamping shut, her body had reverted to a pattern of breathing she'd used in the womb, a pattern that wouldn't work outside the womb, without an umbilical cord. This condition was called persistent fetal circulation, or persistent pulmonary hypertension. They had to try to get her blood vessels to open, which often was just a matter of time. Meanwhile, the respirator forced oxygen to circulate through her lungs. She was also being treated for pneumonitis, a chemical condition of the lungs caused by the toxicity of meconium. It was a lot of information to absorb, but we liked that this doctor assumed we could understand him. Fred and I sat next to each other and studied the sketches and asked questions.

The doctor asked if I'd had difficulties in labor, since babies typically excrete meconium when they are in distress before delivery. When I described the epidural anesthesia with my blood pressure drop and fetal heart rate drop, he said, "Your blood pressure dropped to 72 over 40 and they proceeded with a vaginal delivery?"

"Yes," I said calmly. Should they not have proceeded with a vaginal delivery? We'd discussed emergency C-sections in childbirth class, and been shown the frightening operating room, the screen positioned at the mother's abdomen so she couldn't see the incision. We could have handled that, I thought. Fred was pressing his fingers onto my wrist. The doctor shook his head. We stared at him, but he busily wrote on his pad.

He outlined steps "down the road" in treatment. They would

try to stabilize her, but in the coming days they might have to use pavulon, a paralyzing drug, to prevent her from fighting the respirator. It was an excellent sign that she wasn't on pavulon now. They might decide to use dopamine to raise her blood pressure. A last resort would be a lung bypass machine, called ECMO, at UCSF Hospital, across town.

Fred leaned forward. "What kind of treatment timeframe are we looking at?"

"We aren't."

"If everything went well," I said.

He opened his hands and shrugged. We all just had to wait and see if she lived. Even in my thoughts, "if she lived" sounded overly stark and dramatic and I wanted to substitute more clinical language, such as "wait and see if she responded."

We were visited by the birth certificate registrar, in my hospital room. He had the air of a traveling salesman, proceeding buoyantly from bed to bed with a large briefcase. He pulled up a chair to the side of the bed, took out a form, attached it to a clipboard, and set to work filling in blanks and black-bordered boxes. After we'd named Cade the night before, we hadn't discussed it again. I wasn't sure I liked it. But now we had to give our baby her official name, so we said Cade Emery Leebron, and he filled it in, along with the birth time, 7:24 p.m. July 28, 1992, and birth weight, 7 pounds, 1 ounce. This transaction felt slightly unreal, as if we would eventually receive a piece of paper, but no baby. He put the form in his briefcase, shut it, and clicked the brass latches. "You all call Public Health in three weeks, give or take," he said. "You can go pick it up."

"Great," Fred said.

"Any problems, call me." He snapped his fingers and produced a business card, seemingly out of his sleeve.

"Thank you," I said.

"First baby," he said, rising from his chair. "Hoo boy, nothing like it."

"You bet," Fred said, and the man turned and pretended to knock on the curtain in front of the newest mother's bed. "Knock, knock," he said, and started up again.

Before noon, an X-ray technician wheeled a machine into the nursery and photographed the baby's chest. The breathing tube was still too low. There was a large amount of excess fluid in the right lung, a smaller amount in the left lung. A respiratory therapist pulled the breathing tube and cut it shorter, to four and a half centimeters "from lip to tip," as the therapists said. Cade was agitated intermittently, with worsening oxygen saturation. The neonatologist came to her bedside at two o'clock, after seeing blood oxygen test results. Cade's whole body was swollen. Her oxygen was increased back up to 100 percent, and her breath rate accelerated.

We met with the social worker attached to the ICN, Nina Coronaise. She explained that after I pumped my breastmilk, I could put it in a sterile jar, to be stored in a freezer outside the nursery, and given to Cade when she was ready. I should save every drop, and it would be fed to the baby in the order in which I'd expressed it. She brought us jars filled with sterile water; I would pour out the water and pour in the milk. She also gave us white file labels, to label each jar with Cade's name, and the date and time the milk was expressed. She'd arrange for us to rent an electric breastpump. She asked how long I wanted to stay in the hospital; mothers usually spent at least two nights when their babies were in intensive care. But Fred wasn't allowed to stay with me. I felt desperate for sleep and quiet, and since we lived near the hospital we could come and go easily. Nina said she'd speak with my nurse about an early discharge. We asked if we could stay in one of the parents' rooms that night, but both were reserved. Usually, she said, parents stayed overnight near the time of discharge, to learn about bathing and feeding and medical care. She leaned toward us. "And how is Cade doing?" Her voice had softened.

"We've been given no prognosis," Fred said.

"Critical," I said.

"How difficult for you." Her eyes widened. The sympathy felt real, but also practiced. We straightened in our plastic chairs.

"So I'll check with you about the breastpump?" Fred said.

"Come see me." She crisped up again.

She noted from our conversation that the ICN patient was our first child, a planned pregnancy. We'd lived in San Francisco for a year; almost all of our immediate and extended family were on the East Coast. My mother would be coming to help with the baby after discharge, sooner if needed. Otherwise, our support system consisted of friends. We didn't practice religion. We were both employed. We were coping well, and had discussed the baby's status. We seemed supportive of each other. We were appropriately anxious, and understood that the course of the next few days was unknown.

Fred called my mother, first to report the doctor's information, and then again to hear what the director of medical affairs at her company had said. The director said that it was good she was getting antibiotics. It was good she hadn't been moved to UCSF; major medical centers had more infections, so it was better that she convalesce where she was, unless she worsened. If she wasn't stable or improving, and the doctors would consider moving her within the next 24 hours, then maybe they should consider moving her right away, while she was stronger. If they waited until she was anoxic—not getting oxygen—even with 100 percent oxygen being pumped in by the ventilator, then there was a risk of brain damage, with an immediate evacuation from the nursery, a crisis situation. Better to make a calm move and give the people at UCSF time to review her chart.

"Did I mention that the director used to practice at Bismarck?"

"No," Fred said.

"In pediatrics. I feel I should tell you, he did mention that transfer to another intensive care nursery would be quite expensive for Bismarck," my mother said.

"They'd have to pay for the ECMO," Fred said.

"We need to make sure that pressure doesn't factor in."

Between nursery visits, I was seen by an obstetrician, an anesthesiologist, a nurse. My stitches looked fine. I'd suffered no apparent complications from anesthesia. The nurse injected me with Rhogam, to counteract Rh antibodies. I used the breastpump while sitting up in bed watching the black-and-white television. I watched part of an unidentifiable movie, and part of a talk show on which unattractive teenagers complained about their parents. "She don't listen," a hulking boy said. The pumping hurt, and I kept adjusting the black dial toward "minimum." I felt self-conscious, because the newest mother's husband walked in and out of the room past my bed and was clearly embarrassed, averting his head so far that he might have walked into a wall, a post, a pole. I produced a small amount of thick yellow colostrum and put it in a jar, though I felt foolish saving the few drops. While I ate lunch, I read the hospital guide on newborn care, which felt like a wonderfully normal activity. Of course I had to learn about diapering and bathing and cleaning the umbilical stump. The baby wasn't with me just then, parallel-parked next to the bed in a plastic bassinet cart, but soon she might be with me, and I'd be lifting her up, one hand behind her head, as the guide instructed. I let myself relax and pretend for a few minutes. The day-shift nurse kept asking if I really wanted to go home. "Yes," I said, "yes," and she kept writing in her notes: "Mother still wants to D.C. this p.m." She checked my blood pressure and okayed a six p.m. discharge. In the late afternoon, Fred went home to messenger our freelance job, arrange a rental car, and pick up a breastpump. He would meet me back at the hospital.

I had to call my father, though I didn't want to, didn't have the energy for explaining what I only partially understood. But the last news he'd had was the early good news phone call the night before. My stepmother answered. I tried to keep my voice even. "I wanted to let you know what's happening with the baby. She's not doing very well."

My father picked up the extension, and I described the situation. They were silent. My father said helplessly, "I thought she was doing fine."

"I thought so too." My voice stayed firm. I'd call them with any news. I still didn't dare to call my mother, knowing I would disintegrate into weeping at the sound of her voice. I dressed in the clothes I'd arrived in the day before, feeling too dirty to put on my "going home" outfit. But I wore clean socks; yesterday's were stiff with smears of dried blood. At her desk outside the door, the nurse noted that I talked on the phone and then dressed myself. When I eventually read my medical records for the hospital stay, I was surprised at how carefully the nurses had observed me. The details of the notes revealed a tenderness I hadn't been aware of. At the time, I felt lonely, and annoyed at my physical pains; my baby was the patient, not me.

I piled my belongings on the bed, snapping shut the large plastic bag of supplies the hospital gave me. How comforting it was to have everything I needed: blue waterproof pads to put under me in bed so I wouldn't bleed on my sheets, a sitz bath, extra sanitary pads and belts, medicated wipes, jars of sterile water. At five minutes of six, Fred returned and took my bags to the car.

We were working together smoothly, each of us having accomplished our afternoon tasks, and I felt fairly calm. We went to check on Cade.

Dr. Hanover greeted us in the nursery. Cade was not stabilizing. They'd put her on pavulon, to prevent her from fighting the respirator. She was now paralyzed but conscious. Her eyes were closed, but she wasn't sleeping. To be conscious but paralyzed was painful, so they'd increased the morphine dose. She was also being given dopamine, to raise her blood pressure. The other neonatologist had described these treatments as down the road, but only hours after our conversation they were being used. "What about the lung bypass machine?" I asked.

"That's nothing to think about now," Dr. Hanover said.

"But that's the next step, isn't it?" Fred asked.

"Yes," he said. "If she doesn't respond to this."

"We want to make sure she isn't moved while in crisis," Fred said.

"From what we understand," I said, "it's important to minimize the risk of brain damage."

Hanover crossed his arms more tightly. "You don't need to think about ECMO."

"If you think she might need it," I said, daring myself to make one more statement, "we hope you won't hesitate to move her quickly."

"We will move her if she needs to be moved," he said irritably. "We will call you if we decide to move her."

"I'll check in later to see how she's doing," Fred said.

"Call here anytime," Dr. Hanover said. I looked down; even his ankles were crossed.

The puffy sacs under the baby's eyes had a yellow cast. Her chest moved rapidly up and down, while the rest of her body lay still. I didn't want to leave and yet I wanted to, to rest, and be in our apartment with Fred. It's hard to imagine now that we left the hospital. Surely we should have stayed by her bed, stroking her hand and soothing her through the difficult night. At the time, we felt exhausted, and thought we might as well start the routine we would live for the foreseeable future. We would call, we would come back soon. "Her face looks swollen," I said.

"Around the eyes," Hanover said, gentler now. He placed his large hands on the plastic barrier around her. "She's retaining fluids, but that's okay. We'll just wait and see."

We left him to watch over her. A nurse escorted us to an emergency exit door behind the ICN, and we stepped outside. Fred helped me into the plush-velour front seat of the rental car, and I sat carefully tilted to one side. It seemed I hadn't been outside, hadn't seen trees or traffic or buildings, in a long time. For a few minutes, as we drove home, we felt untethered, and peacefully alone.

3

At home I sat in a chair by the window, watching frisbee players in the park, cars pulling into the gas station. The hospital was a natural setting for a crisis, its waiting areas filled with worried relatives. Technicians wheeled equipment down hallways; nurses' assistants prepared syringes. It didn't seem abnormal to feel upset in a hospital, to hover at a bedside waiting for test results. I hadn't minded too much that the other women in the maternity room had their babies with them, because mine was right down the hall. But to arrive home without Cade was a blow. The carseat waited by the door. The tiny yellow sleeper suit and blanket were still wrapped in a plastic bag, stuffed in the duffel that now sat, zipped shut, at the foot of our bed.

The crib lay in pieces on the floor of the nursery, which we also used as a study. We hadn't wallpapered a room, made curtains, or hung a mobile. Though the middle of my pregnancy went well, it was framed by events that made the chances of a healthy baby feel less than guaranteed: I experienced bleeding in the first trimester, and preterm labor at seven months. The baby clothes Betsy had sent were still in boxes. We'd bought diapers, medical supplies, and a sleeping basket to put next to our bed—the minimum equipment to bring a baby home. We hadn't taken much for granted, as if it would have brought bad luck to presume.

I felt battered. Even my ribs, arms, and neck were sore. I kept looking out the window, feeling sorry for myself. I didn't want to talk to anyone. Planning for uncertainty didn't give any comfort now. I should have made a perfect nursery. Then I could have sat in the rocking chair, surveying a row of silly-faced terrycloth animals and a stack of freshly washed blankets, and I could have cried and cried for my losses. If the baby died, people could say, Can you imagine, she had to pack away all the little clothes. But in our cautious household, the clothes were still packed.

Fred called the nursery, identifying himself as the father of Cade. How strange that sounded. I was the mother of Cade. Across the park and over the hill, we had a baby. The nurse gave the phone to a doctor, who told Fred that they were hyperventilating the baby now, in an effort to improve her oxygenation. She was receiving 120 breaths a minute. She seemed stable for the moment. We imagined her chest fluttering up and down. The triangle of skin under the center of her ribs would rise and deflate, too quickly to count at that breath rate, alterable with the turn of a dial, as if our baby were merely an extension of a machine. Later I slept, on my back, which I hadn't done for months, since that position can reduce the flow of oxygen to the baby.

At 6 a.m. on Thursday, Cade was almost a day and a half old. I called the ICN, and the nurse said that she had experienced a "circular night." She had improved but then worsened, and was "in crisis" between 3 and 4:30 a.m. Two doctors were working on her now. We would have to wait and see. "Okay," I said. "Thank you. We'll come in." I told Fred what she'd said. We didn't like to panic. We'd felt—having made phone calls, dealt with the breastpump, rented a car, talked to doctors and understood them, read the ICN orientation packet—we'd felt that we could handle the business of the day. Take it as it comes. But a crisis happened while we were sleeping, not with her, and we didn't even know what had happened. I was desperate for words. What did "in crisis" mean? I'd read a shelf's worth of pregnancy books, but there was no book for us now, no translation of hospital language. What were the two doctors doing right now? The nurse had seemed to speak reluctantly, uncertainly. Why was I sleeping in my bed while my baby was suffering? Fred enclosed me in his arms so I couldn't see anything, and I cried hard against him. Then we dressed in the clothes we'd thrown on the floor the night before and drove to the hospital.

The nurse was writing on a clipboard. Fred fastened his gown as he walked quickly into the nursery. "How is she?"

"Holding on." She smiled sympathetically. "She had a bad time there."

"Two doctors were working on her?" I asked. The ICN seemed tranquil now, as if nothing had happened. No doctors were present. Cade looked the same as when we'd left the night before— body stilled, eyes closed, head turned to one side, tube in her mouth.

"They worked to improve her oxygen saturation." She pointed to the monitor at the foot of the bed, where blue numbers glowed against a black screen, showing a "sat" rate, or rate of oxygen saturation. They were giving her 100% oxygen, but her body was not absorbing that much. Her body was only oxygenating blood at a minimal rate. The sat number was the rate, and represented an estimate. The real rate was obtained by taking blood via the tube in her umbilicus, and testing it in the lab for oxygen. The nurse's explanation made sense, but I still didn't know what the doctors had done. We only learned much later from reading medical records that they had taken the baby off the ventilator temporarily, and manually resuscitated her. They had discontinued the pavulon and morphine to prevent respiratory failure, then cautiously restarted them at 5:30 a.m.

After they sent her blood down to the lab at 7:30, we waited tensely, not speaking, staring at Cade. Her eyelids were an almost pearlized blue under the warming lights. Her arms lay at her sides, an IV needle taped in place on the back of each hand. Jim Spicer, the respiratory therapist on duty that day, grabbed a slip of paper from the dumbwaiter at 7:55, rushed out of the ICN, then came in and showed it to the nurse. As she wrote down the results, Fred asked her how the numbers were.

She hesitated, then said that the oxygenation could be better, and the blood pressure was low. When she left for a moment I craned around to see her clipboard, but didn't know what the entries meant.

It disturbed me that no one had called us when Cade was in crisis. I didn't want to answer the phone at home and hear someone tell me, Your baby died; I wanted someone to call before that. But we didn't want to make a fuss now, figuring we'd save any unpleasantness for important matters. In the midst of an emergency, who had time to telephone the parents? We were peripheral; if doctors were working on her, we wouldn't even be allowed in the nursery. Still, I'd rather have been at the hospital than sleeping at home. A formal act of panicking might have been as therapeutic as a formal act of grieving, the equivalent of a funeral. We could have paced the halls all night, waiting for someone to emerge and give us news. If she were going, it would help us to hold her hand and say goodbye before she left us. Now we could only sit on our stools in numbness, behaving reasonably, asking logical questions in the daylit room.

Dr. Hanover stepped in and leaned back against the sink, his arms crossed.

"She had a difficult night," I said.

"Yup."

Fred tried. "Do you think she's improving?"

He scratched an eyebrow. "Early to say."

"For the blood gas," I said. "What are good numbers?"

"A lot of parents focus on the numbers," he said. "When they really shouldn't. There's no absolute good number to look for."

What else did we have to focus on? If a lot of parents focused on the numbers, then surely it was out of a natural need. Cade's mouth hung open, her lower lip free of tape; the bottom of her mouth looked as if she'd fallen asleep sitting up. Her top lip and the space between her mouth and nose were plastered with translucent white tape, which held the respirator tube in place. Her chest fluttered up and down. Her face looked puffier, the bags under her eyes yellower. Hanover said she might have a little jaundice, nothing to worry about, and that she was eliminating fluids fairly well.

"Her kidneys work," he said. "That's good." I hadn't considered that her kidneys might *not* work. What else were they worrying about?

The nurse asked us to leave so they could check the baby's breathing tube. We wandered the halls, not knowing that her oxygen index was approaching 40, a number that indicated an 80 percent chance of mortality and warranted the lung bypass machine. As they had done at 3:30 a.m., Jim and another therapist were disconnecting the ventilator, hand-bagging her for a minute with a green rubber balloon to find a rate and pressure at which her lungs would absorb oxygen. The resident examined Cade, advising that the pressure and breath rate should be lowered that day, to avoid life-threatening lung injury. When she'd finished, the therapists hand-bagged for three minutes, then reconnected the baby to the ventilator. We came back in briefly before rounds, the two-hour period when we couldn't be in the nursery; the medical team would assemble before each baby and consider its case. The rounds summary sheet for Cade that day read simply, "Too sick to discuss."

We went home so I could use the breastpump. I took a sitz bath, then lay in bed with an ice-filled glove over my stitches. Fred called our friends George and Denise and asked them to arrange the rental car for another week. He gave them a list of people to phone so we wouldn't get any "Hi, did you have a baby yet?" calls. We called our families with the day's update and gave our other long-distance calls to my mother and sister. Fred called the medical affairs director at my mother's company and they reviewed Cade's worsening condition, the addition of pavulon for paralysis and dopamine for blood pressure maintenance. The director felt that Dr. Hanover was proceeding appropriately. A potential crisis could be inadequate oxygenation coupled with a blood pressure drop, in which case they might use an expander, like albumin, to increase blood volume. "They did give albumin," Fred said, just realizing it.

By late afternoon on Thursday, Cade had not stabilized. She was receiving double-strength dopamine at the maximum dose, to raise her blood pressure. The monitors beeped often, when her pressure or oxygen saturation dipped too low, and Hanover stayed in the nursery, leaning against the sink. Fred and I sat on cushioned stools pulled up to her table. The stools were awkwardly high, like barstools with backs, and stuck out in the small space. Dr. Hanover stood only two feet behind us. Fred turned on his stool. "What's the thinking on ECMO now?"

"We're watching her numbers," Hanover said. "It's a definite possibility." We all stayed silent for a while.

"Is ECMO always the last resort?" I said.

"Depends." He scratched his beard. "The machine allows the lungs to rest and possibly heal." As we learned later, putting a baby on the lung bypass machine involved inserting a tube into the right carotid artery, to drain blood from the right atrium of the heart, running it through an oxygenation process, and returning the blood to the body via the jugular vein.

"So whether you use it depends on what," I said.

"It may not be appropriate, if we're dealing with advanced pneumonitis, for instance."

"Then you wouldn't use the ECMO?" Fred said.

"Antibiotics might be more efficacious." He waved his hand. "No sense talking about hypotheticals."

I'd been focusing on the lung bypass machine, thinking that if she were going to die, they'd put her on that first. We could feel safe because they'd tell us she needed the ECMO; it was a barrier before death. She wouldn't just die at any minute on her warming table. If she didn't stabilize, we would be discussing the risks of transport, familiarizing ourselves with the intensive care nursery at UCSF, keeping our vigil over Cade and her new machine. Obviously there were scenarios I hadn't conceived of. We'd been told Cade might die, and although I'd considered the impact of that idea, I didn't imagine the physical process of my baby dying, her dead body, wouldn't cast that blue shadow over her like a smothering wing. She lay bathed in the perpetual white-gold light of warming lamps, the nursery dim around her. We all watched her chest beating, 74 times a minute now. I shifted my weight. Hanover asked, "Are you getting some rest?"

"Yes."

"You need rest now," he said, with grandfatherly kindness. I flushed at this unexpected attention, and turned back to the baby, distracted. Beyond her table surrounded by equipment was a clear plastic isolette with a tiny infant inside, Baby Ashley. Baby Ashley's mother was sitting on a stool, her yellow-gowned arms stuck through two portholes to change her baby. I thought her clothes were tacky, a bright jungle-print blouse with stretch jeans and new white aerobic sneakers. She wore pastel-colored eyeshadow, blusher and lipstick, and her long brown hair was permed into crinkles. The yellow sterile gown looked almost as ugly on her as it did on me.

I wondered why Cade wasn't in an isolette, like Ashley. Maybe only preemies lived in them, being too fragile to come outside. When Hanover ducked out for a minute, I asked the nurse why Cade was on a table. So they could get to her quickly if they had to, she explained. And the warming lights regulated her body temperature better than an incubator, whose portholes allowed the air inside to heat and cool.

I'd taken her being on this table as a good sign, evidence that she was more robust than other babies. My assumptions were being corrected too often, and I began to feel off kilter. I remembered when my sister tripped and fell flat as a child, cracking her cheekbone on the neighbor's brick terrace. Two doctors had questioned me separately and I'd realized—oh!—that they thought someone had hit her. And I recalled finding my grandmother's lovely white teeth in a motel-room glass. Recent love letters from a highschool girl in the underwear drawer of a man I lived with. These moments occurred years apart so I didn't have to feel bewildered; I could still be at home in the world. In this hospital, I was making too many mistakes. How could I get better at knowing what the hell was going on?

The nursery consisted of three rooms in a row, with dividing walls of glass from waist level up, and open doorways between rooms. We were in the first room on the left. I could see only into the middle room, which held three babies in incubators. So Cade was the only baby on a warming bed. Was she the sickest one, sicker than the red-skinned babies half her size? I couldn't believe those tiny sick-looking babies had a better chance than she did. When Hanover came back in, I said quietly, "So I just want to know, it's very possible she may not make it." I knew he thought that was an unnecessary question. Fred probably thought it was a stupid question, which it was. Both of them looked for a long moment at me, the dull one who needed everything spelled out.

Hanover said, "She might not."

Outside the nursery, I told Fred we should tell our parents they could come and see her. I felt panicked with guilt over my mother. She wanted to come, and I'd kept her away. I'd hesitated to have my mother come help with the baby, fearing that Fred might be pushed aside. Fred and I were extremely close; my mother and I were extremely close; but Fred and my mother still had a certain distance between them. With Cade ill, I felt even more strongly that Fred and I needed to lock together, and that we couldn't afford to have him feel left out. But it was my mother's first grandchild, the first grandchild on my side of the family. Cade might die and my mother wouldn't have seen her. I insisted that we call all of the grandparents.

I had begun to believe, too, that if Cade died unseen, it would be only Fred's and my loss. She wouldn't seem real to anyone else. And maybe if Cade died I could forget her, too. I needed a collective memory to give mine authority. Fred and I had sat up in bed and decided that if she died we would take a long trip to Indonesia. Her death would be a terrible episode in our lives that we would recover from; maybe we would have no children, then, and become minor tragic figures, expatriate writers with a dead baby. There was a self-important glamour in that, an allure to the idea of drinking ourselves into oblivion on a beach somewhere. We would survive our child's death, more or less. But we were here. The baby was still alive.

My mother wasn't home, and I didn't want to leave an unsettling message. Fred reached his mother. He said, "Hi. She's not doing so great. We thought—" Then he started to cry, the only time I saw him cry during this, and he blindly pushed the phone at me. I explained that we didn't want people coming out for us, but that if they wanted to see Cade, they should feel free to come. I really couldn't bear the thought of people snuffling and hugging me, talking about me in lowered voices while I lay resting in the afternoon, the bedroom blinds pulled down. Stiff and stoical was my preferred posture. Carol was matter-of-fact, as always, so it was possible for me to remain composed. She had been pragmatic when her husband lay near death for several months in a Milwaukee hospital. She researched his heart condition and all the surgeries, and questioned the specialists who worked on him. She knew his treatments, and several times had to correct the nurses when they gave him the wrong kind or amount of medication. She was tough. I liked talking to her.

When I called my father, my stepmother answered; he wasn't home. It was eight o'clock on the East coast, and she'd had a few drinks, which wasn't unusual for that time of night. I liked to call them on Saturday afternoons, after my father had played tennis, before the cocktail hour. I made my statement, and rolled my eyes at Fred as she started asking questions. This wasn't about my father, she said, this was about me, wasn't it? *I* needed him to come. *He* didn't need to come. What would she tell my father when he got home, I wondered. She persisted—wasn't this really about me? What did *I* need? Yes, the request was for me, but it was also for him, I tried to explain. If my dad didn't get the chance to meet his first grandchild, he might feel sorry. I hated her booze-slowed psychologizing, as if anyone had time to figure it all out just then.

Dr. Hanover wrote notes in Cade's chart at six o'clock that evening. The baby had been alive for almost two days. He must have been tired. "Have been in attendance since 0800," he began. His notes, usually in almost-fluid prose, were cryptic scrawls. "Paralyzed," he wrote, and "PFC—severe." Oxygenation was difficult. "Will prob need TX in next 1–2 d," he wrote, indicating the need for a blood transfusion. He described us as "in to visit/touch for long intervals." The equation of visit and touch is telling—he always wanted us to touch her, even as alarms went off and nurses glared at us for disturbing her. He believed in the laying on of hands. We were aware of our baby's "grave condition, without much room to spare should oxygenation decrease—also aware of possibility of transfer to ECMO if condition worsens." He wrote sideways in the margin, maybe to add a hopeful note, "lung fluids much clearer!"

As we put on yellow gowns in the anteroom, Fred heard someone in the hall. "Alan," he said. "Alan." He walked out and hugged a colleague of his. I thought, *It's an angel.* My shoulders dropped from their tense position. We hadn't seen anyone we knew in three days, and here was Alan Watahara, who loved my husband, who had helped us get an apartment when we returned from Guatemala, who had hired Fred at a Berkeley institute, who drove a battered VW Bug and worked for almost no pay. He carried a large paper grocery bag filled with food. He thought he was intruding; he handed the bag to Fred and said, "I'm sorry, I don't want to bother you." He stepped backwards. We stepped forward.

"Wait," Fred said. "How are you?"

"How are *you?*" Alan said.

"Hanging in," Fred said.

"And the baby?"

"Still with us. You could probably see her from the doorway."

"No," Alan said, waving away the idea. "How's mom doing?"

"Fine," I said. "I've had some sleep."

Alan spoke in a low voice. "The strangest thing happened—on my way here, I ran into friends, who also have a baby in the ICN."

"You're kidding," I said. There were only six or seven babies in the whole unit.

"No. A boy born with Down's Syndrome, with an incomplete colon."

"He must be in the other end room, because we haven't seen him."

"Did they know about the Down's?" Fred said.

"No, they didn't." We considered this. "Call me, you guys, if there's anything."

At the end of the hall, he stopped and began speaking in Japanese with his friends. It seemed in accordance with Alan's generosity that he should be comforting not just one, but two sets of parents. As for us, we were happy to have seen someone we knew and to have acted normally. We were still ourselves.

In the ICN we were learning more from the nurses, some of whom explained numbers and monitors to us. Cade had many different nurses during her stay, and we often felt disconcerted to walk in and see an unfamiliar one. That night a new nurse taught us about pH and $PaCO_2$, the measurements of acidity and carbon dioxide in Cade's blood. Blood gas tests revealed these numbers, which we remembered watching for Fred's father. When the numbers came within a certain range, the blood vessels in the lungs might dilate again and allow blood to pass through. Now the ventilator forced air into her lungs, and the longer she was on the ventilator—especially with high concentrations of oxygen, which damaged lung tissue—the higher the risk became that the ventilator would blow a hole in her lung. A hole in the lung, the nurse explained, could be fatal if it happened outside a hospital. You stop breathing, and surgery is required immediately. If Cade had a hole, it would set her back, but it probably wouldn't cause her to die.

How harsh all of the treatment was on her body—the ventilator, the toxic oxygen, the pavulon that paralyzed her, the morphine. Her whole body appeared yellowish to me, especially where fluid had accumulated to form bags under her closed eyes. Her hair, never washed or brushed, matted darkly on her scalp. An IV had been moved to the top of her head, and, out of a mass of tape plastered at all angles, the needle stuck up at a tilt.

"Good veins up there," the nurse commented. "Have you thought about a music box? Some parents bring in a tape player or music box."

"We'll get one," Fred said. "Today." He looked as stricken as I felt—we hadn't thought of it. Baby Ashley's isolette was decorated with puffy stuffed animals, and pictures taped to the sides. Every time we left Cade we felt as if we were abandoning her, and we'd been leaving nothing of ourselves behind. Toys and pictures seemed absurd—she couldn't move, her eyes were closed. Yet if these things could possibly help, she should have them. I wondered what else ICN parents did that we had overlooked.

The nurse invited us to stay while she did a blood gas, which made us feel welcome, as if we belonged there. She untwisted a plastic cap from the end of the skinny tube coming from Cade's umbilicus, and screwed on a syringe. Bright blood came up into the curling tube, looped a loop, and flooded the small chamber of the syringe. She detached the syringe and laid it on a tray, recapped the tube, shook the syringe, dropped it in a plastic bag which she sealed and labeled, placed it on a bed of ice in a plastic tub, and carried it to the dumbwaiter in the next room. She called the lab to say it was coming. The results would be sent in half an hour.

In the hallway, Fred slowed his pace to walk beside me. I was still bleeding, and carried bulky hospital-issued pads and wipes with me in an old canvas bag, along with a disposable breast pumping kit to use with the hospital's pump in case we wanted to stay. When we moved from place to place, I walked in short, slow steps. Fred would drop me off at the door of the hospital or our apartment and then go park. I sat with my weight on one side because of the episiotomy, easing myself gingerly onto the nursery stool. I tried to do a warm sitz bath once a day to encourage healing, stay off my feet, and sleep when I could. Tiny red bruise-spots had appeared in a row below my eyebrows, like a bizarre eye makeup, from the strain of pushing in labor.

In the closed snack bar, Fred unstacked two chairs and pulled them up to a table. We lifted the food out of Alan's bag, and exclaimed over it: fried chicken, green salad, a round loaf of bread, cookies, mineral water, an egg-sized chocolate truffle in a shiny white box. We ate everything with our hands, by light that slanted in from the hall, hardly speaking because we were hungry. We laughed over the image of Alan standing in front of the deli counter at a grocery store, ordering chicken and wildly picking up everything else he saw around him.

Cade seemed more stable than the night before; the lab tests indicated no change. Her blood pressure had improved, and her dopamine dosage had been reduced. "Maybe she's turning the corner." The nurse tilted her head, inviting us to agree.

"Hmmm," Fred said, and I said, "Good," but we didn't let ourselves believe her.

I called my mother from a hospital payphone, anxious to reach her, since I'd already told the other grandparents they could come. She said she'd get there as soon as she could, probably Saturday.

"Cade is going to make it," she said. "I just know it. She's seven pounds, so strong!"

"But Mom," I said, annoyed. "Only full-term babies suffer from meconium aspiration. The smaller ones can't *have* a bowel movement."

"I still think she'll be fine," she said. "She's got good genes." I gave her a loud sigh. She would obviously say whatever illogical thing she could think of to convince me. I didn't want to be convinced that the baby would live, demanding instead that my mother accept reality and listen to me. I wavered from serenity to fretfulness to despair.

I complained about Dr. Hanover's unwillingness to tell us much. He acted evasive, defensive, condescending. What if he were defensive because he didn't know what he was doing? How could we find out about his professional reputation? Mom said she would make some calls in the morning and learn what she could; if he wasn't a good doctor, we would find another one.

I didn't think in large amounts of time, then. I thought in minutes, in hours. When I was pregnant I could think in years, of putting a child on the schoolbus, of walking in the woods and collecting leaves to press in a book. I used to have a leaf-pressing kit. "Having a child will bring out the best in us," I'd said to Fred. We'd be curious again, we'd invent rituals to mark the seasons, we'd rent a cabin some summer and teach ourselves to fish. Now time had shrunk. I felt shut down, alert only to physical sensation, facts and numbers. Was it shock, or fear, or a practiced autopilot?

I'm sure some of my stubborn inhabitance of the moment came from practice in childbirth class of focusing on the present contraction, the present pain, and not panicking about the fifty increasingly painful contractions yet to come. This was added to years of practice at staying relatively serene, after having been diagnosed with manic depression: I was hospitalized in November of my highschool senior year, at a psychiatric facility. I was on an open ward, with other suicidal types, heavily drugged schizophrenics, and a couple of incorrigible alcoholics. The ward felt safer than my highschool culture, which crackled with sex and heavy drinking around a nucleus of academic work. The academic work was fine, except for my certainty that no good college would accept me. My parents drove me for college tours and interviews from Duke in the south to Wesleyan in the north, and all the while I felt like a tainted specimen, too small, too shy, too unathletic. My private highschool was full of healthy children of the rich, who played soccer and lacrosse, and vacationed at Aspen; they'd frightened me when I'd first seen them as eighth-graders, in their bright madras clothes and silver braces. Now I am curious about them, in their adult forms as New York City stockbrokers and interior decorators. With their stone houses in New Jersey, their scotch, their extramarital affairs, their antique furniture, golden retrievers—they've become the parents of children I knew, the parents who scrutinized me, an outsider, as the most likely conduit to anything nasty their children might be indulging in. Their children had already secured a place in the world. Who was I?

Boys liked me for a girlfriend, and so I got invited in. The story of the next years doesn't belong; it is enough to say that while I made friends I still have today, and worked hard for inspiring teachers, I also engaged in an excessive social life and became repetitively, but not terminally, self-destructive. One day, I met for one hour with a psychiatrist and was committed to the hospital for observation. (My mother must have been relieved; having a daughter who swallows all of the Tylenol in the house and then calls you at work to tell you so is surely no fun.) And it was fine there, with many amusements—making leather bracelets, writing

poems about feelings, doing jumping jacks in the gym with people on thorazine who couldn't even clap their hands together.
When I left on a day pass to watch a soccer game at school, I
couldn't wait to get back to the hospital, where everyone felt
uncomfortable with themselves. And yet I wouldn't ever want to
do it again. I was still a child at the time, and my failures could be
covered up by my school headmaster, who attested in my college
file that I had missed school due to pneumonia. My weaknesses
could be addressed by my mother, who wouldn't leave me alone.
I slept for a while in the bedroom next to hers, a warm narrow
room filled with her old, sustaining books by Virginia Woolf and
Doris Lessing.

My discharge diagnosis was manic depression. Lithium had
no effect on me, but the clinic psychiatrist told me I'd not live a
normal life without medication, and prescribed antidepressants.
The doctor was wrong, of course—my medicated life lasted only
two months. It ended when I despairingly swallowed a whole bottle
of antidepressants (with minimal effort since they looked exactly
like tiny, spicy red-hot candies) soon after my boyfriend told me
he had a crush on someone else at school.

I distrusted my hospital doctors, who could label me so per-
emptorily and absolutely as manic-depressive. And while their
diagnosis felt wrong, I also distrusted myself, knowing that every
feeling of euphoria would be followed by a crash, knowing, over
the years, that Plath and Woolf didn't commit suicide because of
a new, especially profound depression, but because of the sheer
tedium of repetitive suicidal desire. *It's happening again,* I would
think bitterly, as I sat in my apartment in one city or another, unable to pick up the telephone or eat or take a shower or vacuum
or change my clothes. So during the in-between times, which gradually have stretched farther and farther, I'd always think, *even keel.*
Keep the keel in the water. I pictured a white sailboat keel in cold

greenish water, the brine of Nova Scotia of an Elizabeth Bishop poem, or of Maine where my dad took us sailing. If we didn't keep the proper balance on the boat, it would heel to the side, and the keel, the long planar sharkfin of it, would threaten to whoosh to the surface as we all got dumped overboard. Falling into water is fine. But falling toward the extremes of what's now labeled bipolar illness is not. So I'd tell myself, Don't scream, don't shout with joy, don't drink too much. Much happiness has come to me this way. This willful numbing of emotion cannot be wrong or sad. I still drink a glass of wine, sing when my friend plays the guitar, and love my husband; I just don't drink the whole bottle, sleep with strangers, or regard razorblades as instruments of release from a shameful life. Sometimes emotions, as fashionable as they are, don't help me. When my baby was in the hospital, I often retreated to a more primary source of being: my body. What did I see, hear, and touch, and what did it mean? Isn't this how infants learn the world?

That night, while we slept, our baby opened her eyes in the nursery. The overhead warming lamps must have been very bright for her. She was immediately given pavulon and morphine, and within 30 seconds, she closed her eyes again.

My father woke us in the morning by seven, to say that he'd be arriving in San Francisco in the evening. I was stunned. Except for our visits to him near Christmas, he had governed as a father from afar, ensconced in a comfortable house with his wife and stepdaughter. Our relationship was almost not a relationship, though he had been warmer and more attentive during my pregnancy. He and Maureen had visited while I was confined to bed in June. They sat uncomfortably in our garage-sale chairs. We discussed their trip and the weather. I'd accepted that my father and I, who looked alike and were both stonily stubborn, had already passed our best years together. When I was a child I knew he loved me, knowledge that could last my whole life, even if he didn't like me much anymore. But he'd made efforts during the visit, reading the paper and watching tennis on TV, buying me a 50-foot telephone cord, bringing in takeout food. He seemed to be taking his grandfather's role quite seriously. I failed to give Maureen any credit: as I discovered later, it was Maureen who had insisted they come to the hospital right away, buying airline tickets as my father mentally reviewed his work calendar for a less-busy day.

When we arrived at the hospital, as became our habit, one of us rushed in to see Cade while the other deposited chilled breast-milk in the nursery freezer and piled our jackets and bags in a parents' room. I hurried to the nursery first, and Dr. Hanover stopped me in the anteroom. "People are calling me from Washington," he said evenly. "I can't give out details of this case, it's confidential information." He slapped down a manila folder on the desk. "You know that."

I didn't step backwards, though I wanted to. "I'm sorry."

"Who do you want me to talk to? Why don't you ask me what you want to know?" He was getting more and more nettled. "Who is in Washington?" he said loudly, and the unit assistant looked up at him. "I've got the head of hospital calling me and asking to be briefed on this case. Who is ordering these telephone calls?"

"My mother is in Washington," I said. "I asked her to get some information."

"I will be glad," he sniffed, thoroughly put out, "to speak with her personally after rounds."

"Thank you." I turned away from him to wash my hands, and he picked up his file and opened it.

At home during rounds, I called my sister, who was in Washington, visiting our mother before graduate film school started again in Los Angeles. I had to talk to her, but I didn't want to, I was too tired. With Mom I talked facts, with Cecily interpretation, and I couldn't articulate my feelings yet. When she'd been ill earlier in the summer, she'd gone to the hospital over and over for invasive tests with disturbing results, and I couldn't really feel what that was like, I could only wish she didn't have to feel it. How could she feel what this was like for me? *I* didn't even know what this was like for me, or what it even was. A terrible thing was happening to me, and yet it wasn't happening to *me*, it was happening to my baby. "I'm so tired," I said.

"I know," she said. "Mom keeps saying the baby will be fine."

"Nobody knows if the baby will be fine," I said vehemently.

"She's driving me crazy."

I laughed. "Is she clicking her nails on her coffee cup?" Our mother always signaled us when we'd lingered too long at breakfast and should be getting out and about.

"She'll hardly sit down."

"Poor Mom."

"I know." Cecily sighed. "So you're going back and forth to the hospital?"

"All day. We're in a routine."

"You're busy."

"It's good. We have very little time to think." It was odd that she happened to be at our mother's house instead of her apartment in Los Angeles; I felt flung back in time to when she was in high school and I'd left for college. I'd call in with all my big news from the world, like how many slides we had to memorize for the art history exam, or what I'd done on Saturday night. "I do ice-packs and sitz baths, and there's breastpumping. Fred sterilizes the pump every morning."

"I am never having a baby," she said firmly.

As we talked, our mother was at work, waiting in a hallway of the Senate Office Building for a hearing to finish. She called the

Bismarck representative in Washington again, who told her that he'd heard the situation was critical, and the baby might not live. If it were him, he said, he'd get on a plane for California. Yes, she told him, she'd already reserved the first seat available. When she recounted this conversation to me months later, I was surprised that she'd known how ill Cade was. I thought she didn't realize it, that she wasn't listening to me. I was also startled that the hospital's official word had been that the baby might not live. The doctors and nurses and respiratory therapists went about their work calmly, of course, since critical illness was routine for them in this nursery. They never brought up death, and I'd begun to feel as if I were extreme or hysterical to focus on the possibility. In the ICN, we seemed to exist in a futureless present tense, in which we could discuss medications and strategies, but never a prognosis.

After rounds, Baby Ashley's mother sat on a stool beyond Cade's table, her back to Ashley's isolette. Dr. Hanover faced her from a low chair. We usually minded our own business in the nursery, not wandering around to look at other babies, not listening too closely to the nurses discussing cases, or weekend plans, not often meeting the eyes of other parents as they came and went. We acted the same way everyone did. All of the families seemed to crave privacy, to create an invisible perimeter around their baby's area, bounded by respirators, IV carts, and a nurse in a chair. But we could not help overhearing Baby Ashley's mother say, "Part of her brain is missing?"

"The tests seem to indicate," Hanover said, and we couldn't hear the rest.

The mother straightened up on her stool; she looked pinned to it. "Which part?"

"It's not a very important part," Hanover said affably. "It's the kind of lack you can make up for by reading her lots of books, that sort of thing." I saw her struggling to formulate questions, and I knew her struggle. Hanover would give a morsel of information and I would think, *What is the question? What is the question I can ask that will elicit more information? If I don't ask a precise question, he won't tell me anything.* She asked something about the cerebral cortex. I knew those words, but only as I heard her say them; I couldn't have summoned them up and asked that question. Where was her husband, and why did Hanover look as relaxed as if he were discussing the Sunday paper? Read her lots of books. I was ashamed to have thought of Ashley's mother as tacky. She persisted with questions while the doctor looked blandly back at her.

My mother was silent when I called from home to tell her Dad was coming that night. She would come the next night, Saturday, and leave Monday morning. Grandparents' visiting hours were from 1–2 and 7–8 every day. One grandparent could be in the room with one parent. It made me tense to think about portioning out the time between my father, his wife, and my mother.

My mother said, "The director has asked around about Dr. Hanover, and the word is, he has an excellent reputation."

"Really?"

"Critically ill babies from other Bay Area hospitals are often sent to him."

This news gave me tremendous hope. If he could save babies that other hospitals couldn't handle, then Cade was getting the best possible care. "Who cares if the man won't talk?" I said lightly.

"Exactly," my mother said. "As long as he saves our baby."

We rushed back to the hospital to be there at 7:24 p.m. Cade would be three days old, and Fred had decided that we should be with her at her birth time every day; I had only just caught on. We quickly scrubbed and gowned and pulled up two high stools to her table, one of us on each side. I sat between her table and the door, pulled up close so people could walk behind me. On the other side of the table, Fred sat with his stool carefully placed among a nest of wires. To his right was the ventilator, a blue box on a stand, with digital readouts of breaths being given per minute, percentage of pure oxygen, and something called "PEEP." The blood pressure and heart rate monitor hung over Fred's left shoulder. On the wall, the pink-and-white "I'm a Girl" card with Cade's birth information now had "Dad - Fred" written on it. We softly touched Cade's arms and said, as we always did, "Hi honey, it's Mom and Dad. We're here." We told her she'd made it through three whole days, and how brave she was, and that grandparents were coming to see her the next day. Her head was turned so she was facing Fred. We took out the things we'd brought for her: a photograph of the two of us that my mother had taken at Christmas, when I was nine weeks pregnant, in which Fred has his arms around me, and we are leaning back in a restaurant banquette, looking happy; a black-and-white terrycloth puppy with a red bow around its neck, chosen because the nurse said babies see only contrast, not colors, at first; and a wind-up music box. We taped the photo to the clear plastic barrier she faced, and placed the puppy below it. We put the music box out of the way at a bottom corner of the bed. I felt much better having brought these tokens, as if they would give her comfort, as if we could bring pieces of home to her.

The intensive care nursery couldn't have been less like home, with its sterile paper gowns, electronic sounds, equipment housed in metal boxes. Yet it was a human place. Ashley's nurse shook out her blond hair and talked with Ashley's mom about aerobics class; another nurse called his little girl at home to say goodnight. While Fred and I stared at Cade as if willing her to wake up—though medicine, not sleep, kept her eyes closed—we listened to the almost inaudible sound of a country-western song being played at low volume in the anteroom, the unit assistant tapping time with his pencil on the desk.

4

Jim Spicer, the respiratory therapist, seemed uncomfortable talking with us about Cade's progress, or lack of progress. His eyes kept darting to the side, and I'd automatically look where he was looking, but nothing was there. When the blood gas results came back, he avoided us, ducking his head, busying himself at the cabinet. *How annoying he is,* I thought, and then, *So the guy doesn't like to give bad news.* We didn't understand yet that Jim was setting the ventilator and helping to determine what the blood gas results would be. He wasn't just delivering the bad news—he was creating it. It wasn't his fault that the baby was ill, or that she wasn't improving, but he felt responsible.

We asked him questions about the ventilator: What did it mean that she was getting 100% oxygen? How many breaths per minute was a good amount? What was PEEP? They were still playing with the numbers to try to stabilize her, he explained. There was no optimal number to look for; we were aiming for stability, achieved through a combination of percentage of pure oxygen, assisted breaths per minute, and PEEP, which was the pressure at which the oxygen was given. I asked, "The higher the pressure the more of a risk of a hole in her lung?"

"Yes," he said, looking down. He looked up. "But it's really good she hasn't had that problem so far." We all knew that the longer Cade was on the ventilator, the higher the risk became. He stepped away to check his other ventilator babies.

Fred and I studied the monitors. Her heart rate was low, but they'd told us not to worry about that. Her blood pressure was low, but not too low, they said, though Jim described it as unstable in his notes that night. Her face was getting puffier, the eyelids, the sacs under the eyes. Her nose had swollen, her cheeks become higher, though it was difficult to see them because of the tape around the ventilator tube. She appeared yellower, too, in her face. Her stomach looked pale yellow. Maybe she just had the golden skin of Fred's family instead of the pink of mine. "Does she look yellow to you?" I asked Fred.

"Somewhat." We noticed the tiny blue bruises, marked with purple pinpricks, on each of her hands.

"There was redness at the sites," the nurse said. "So we moved the IVs." She stood up. "I saw a leg move."

We stared at her legs, but they remained still. Even though we dreaded seeing Cade move, we also wanted to see. What would her leg be like when it wasn't splayed flat, bent at the knee, immobile?

The nurse invited us to stay while she gave pavulon. She injected it into one of the IVs. She moved quickly but without seeming to rush.

"You're so calm about everything," I said.

She laughed as she sat down. "I have five kids at home. All boys." She talked to us normally, not as if we were to be pitied.

We overheard Jim talking to a nurse in the next room about

traveling to Thailand, and when he returned to check on Cade we asked him about it. His wife was Thai, he said, and he visited her family in Bangkok and played golf.

"We lived in Chiang Mai for three months," Fred said.

"Pretty up there. What were you doing?"

"Writing," I said. He raised his eyebrows, which were black, in contrast to his blond hair. Did he dye his hair? "Fred had a fellowship."

"Where did you guys live?"

"Near the drama school. Rongreen Nataseen," I said, in my best Thai accent. We'd traveled in pick-up truck taxis around the city; Fred had perfected his pronunciation of Tha Phae Gate, so we could get into town, and I'd worked on our street name, so we could get home.

"There's an excellent golf course out by the airport."

"I had no idea," I said.

"You ever get up to Mae Si?"

"Sure," Fred said. "We stayed in a dump." Our hotel room had resembled a shoebox that had been used for an ashtray. To escape it, we'd gone to the Frontier Saloon, Mae Si being on the Burmese border, and gotten drunk while watching teenage transvestite Elvis impersonators sing "Blue Suede Shoes" and dance with each other.

Jim said, "What about that resort outside of town?"

"They were building it," Fred said.

"Four diamonds. It's supposed to have a sweet course." He practiced a golf swing, expertly avoiding all of the monitors.

"I'd love to get back there," Fred said emphatically. Fred had first left home when he was 13, as a summer exchange student in Germany, and he'd been leaving ever since. He'd lived in Denmark, and Spain, and Singapore. He'd traveled in Peru, China, Indonesia, and Morocco by himself. His itinerant nature attracted me when we first met, on orientation day for a graduate writing program; he dressed like he'd just come from an international clothing bazaar, in soft Spanish boots, old Levi's corduroys, and a black cotton shirt from Hong Kong with an orange dragon embroidered on the back.

Across the warming bed from me now, he looked less exotic, in a button-down shirt under his yellow gown, and handsome wire-framed glasses. When we met, he'd worn blue plastic glasses with tinted lenses, which my mother said made him look like a drug dealer. He'd worn his curly hair long; now I regularly cut it short. Had I, wishing to be as adventurous as he was, instead cut his life into a conventional shape? He was 31 years old, living in a comfortable apartment, a new father. He worked in fund development and strategic planning for nonprofits. We both taught college composition part-time and did freelance writing. We walked in the park. We rented videos.

I remembered waking up on the northbound train to Chiang Mai as we rode through a valley of green ricefields. I'd said, It looks like Vietnam, realizing that all I'd seen of Vietnam were movies shot in Thailand. We used to drink Mekong whiskey at night in our rented house and play cards. During the steamy afternoons, we wrote in the air-conditioned U.S. Information Service library, and since we dressed conservatively, not wanting to offend the women who cooked in the street markets where we ate, everyone thought we were CIA. I looked at Jim and smiled, thinking of us all there—Fred and I walking along the road, and Jim pulling a golf bag onto the course.

"When I come back she'll be in fine condition," he said.

Dr. Hanover had come into the nursery, and was leaning against the sink. "The textbook case," he said, "turns around suddenly and recovers."

"Well then, I hope she's a textbook case." I tried to match his

quietly jovial style. It didn't help to seem anxious or aggressive—
when Hanover got defensive he clammed up altogether. Even his
eyes seemed to recede, becoming pale-blue points behind his
glasses.

My father had left a message on our machine, from the
Denver airport. He and Maureen had missed their first flight, a
direct Newark-San Francisco one. The next flight had stopped in
Denver, but when it continued, a man had had a heart attack and
the flight turned back. They might get a midnight flight to Los
Angeles and come up in the morning, he said, his voice flat and
exhausted. He sounded wretched. It occurred to me that everyone
was wretched, our parents, our families, our friends.

Our friends Shane and Jane had left an envelope at our door,
with three medical journal articles inside. Shane practiced psy-
chiatry at UCSF and had volunteered to get us information on
meconium aspiration syndrome and persistent pulmonary hypertension. One copy showed Jane's watch next to the page; it read
7:40. They were late for an eight o'clock engagement, they were
leaving the next morning for a two-week camping trip, and they'd
gone to a bewildering medical library for us, an errand for which
we had no time or energy.

We talked to Fred's sister Betsy, whom I admired for raising
four children and teaching full-time; now I felt most admiring of
her fortitude with her son Jonathan, dealing with weeks of intensive care after his birth, and a first year when Jonathan didn't move
his eyes or limbs, didn't vocalize or babble. Then there had been
years of discouraging language and motors skills tests, specialists,
and therapy sessions. I didn't know many details of Jonathan's
case. Where had I been when he was born? We were in graduate
school at Iowa. Why didn't I know more? How could I have been
so detached? I was embarrassed to reveal my ignorance with too

many questions. Betsy asked if our friend had given us ECMO research, and since he hadn't, she promised to go to the medical library the next day. There were questions about the purpose and efficacy of the lung bypass machine, and we ought to be able to make an informed decision.

We cleared off our work table. Fred brought out containers of food, left by Denise at our door that morning, and we sat down to eat dinner and read. The articles were written for doctors, not parents, and though I didn't know all of the terms, it was a relief to get the information straight.

One of the articles said, "Before birth, meconium aspiration may be prevented by early recognition of the compromised fetus and appropriate intervention." I read that aloud.

Fred said, "Listen to this—'Severe pulmonary involvement due to aspiration of meconium can be almost completely prevented by effective tracheal suction immediately after birth.'"

"The other article says it, too." I flipped a page. "'Most meconium aspiration occurs with the onset of air breathing, hence the success of immediate suctioning at birth.'" Babies could inhale a small amount of meconium in utero, but it wasn't until the umbilical cord was cut and they started to breathe through their mouths that they would inhale forcefully and deeply. "Did she suction the baby?"

"Not that I recall."

We thought about Dr. Greg saying, "What do I do now?", and the nurse, who couldn't see the baby from where she stood near my head, saying, "Put her up with mom." Dr. Greg had cut the cord by then. How many breaths had the baby taken before being suctioned? She was on my chest, she looked at me, she blinked, she was carried away.

"Why did the nurse take her out?" I said.

"She was turning purple."

"I didn't even notice that. Then what did she do?"

"Carried her through that central area, where the monitors are. There were people there, talking and standing around, and the nurse said, I need some help here. But nobody moved. We went into a dark little room and she said, Get the lights."

"You had to find the light switch?"

"Yes. The room was cold. She put a tube down the baby's throat and sucked to bring up meconium."

"Gross," I said.

"No," Fred said impatiently. "It's special tubing—you put one end down, suck on another end, and the meconium collects in a third branch."

"How many breaths do you think she took between delivery and suctioning?"

"It was at least a minute, probably two."

"Sixty breaths?"

"Easily," Fred said. We looked at each other grimly. With every breath the meconium spread more distantly into the lungs, past where it could be suctioned out. Meconium was toxic; one account compared meconium hitting the lung tissue to a flash burn.

"I didn't even touch her really, and I had meconium on my hand!" I said, upset now. "Shouldn't the doctor have noticed she had meconium on her?"

"Sure," Fred said.

"They said they suctioned out *lots* of meconium, right?"

"An extraordinary amount, they told me in the ICN."

We read that all delivery rooms should be prepared for immediate suction, intubation, and oxygenation of an asphyxiated infant. The baby should be suctioned by the obstetrician as soon as the head was delivered. The doctors knew there was meconium if the amniotic fluid was stained green or brown. My amniotic fluid was clear when they broke my waters at 3:00, but epidural anesthesia was administered at 4:15, after which my blood pressure dropped and the baby's heart rate dropped. Fetal distress often caused a full-term baby to have a bowel movement, and the baby suffered measurable distress. Shouldn't they have been prepared for the possibility of meconium? I felt hatred for Dr. Greg, for her saying "What do I do now?", for her not knowing how to stitch me up.

I remembered an exchange between Greg and the delivery nurse hours after the birth, when I was still in the delivery room, and the nurse held the clipboard out to Greg and said, "Sign here." As she handed it to Greg, she pointed with her pen and said, "We just made the Apgars 4 and 5, from 3 and 5."

"Really?" Dr. Greg had said, as if she weren't at all interested, and she signed her name and went out. I'd thought, how do you change Apgar scores? These scores assigned to the newborn at one and five minutes of life rate appearance and breathing on a scale of zero to ten. How do you change the scores hours after the event? I wondered what else I would remember, or learn. Cade was three days old. I felt reluctant to read one more word, dreading the painfulness of the learning process. I wanted to understand everything wholly and immediately.

"I guess we should have requested a C-section due to fetal distress," Fred said.

"Or at least asked, Is there suctioning and intubation equipment in the room?" I laughed in disbelief.

"Next baby, we'll know," Fred said. We were kidding, but we were serious. If only we'd asked, if we'd known what to ask, if we'd been more on top of the situation.

According to all of the charts and diagrams in the articles, Cade had proceeded to the worst possible point. On an arrow flowchart, she was "aspiration," lower righthand corner. Another flowchart showed the options after aspiration, including peripheral airway occlusion and proximal airway occlusion, but Cade had bypassed those less serious conditions and passed down the right side of the chart, through pneumonitis, hypoxemia and acidosis, to persistent pulmonary hypertension of newborn, in the lower righthand corner. She was at the end, after the last arrows. Now what? The chances for mortality and injury remained high, though babies who died usually did so in the first 72 hours. She'd made it three days.

We finally discovered what ECMO stood for: extracorporeal membrane oxygenator. I imagined an iron lung, our baby swallowed by a huge metal cylinder. PEEP stood for positive end-expiratory pressure, the pressure exerted by the ventilator. Pressure had to be high enough to force oxygen into the lungs, but as low as possible to prevent a rupture. Infants with severe MAS frequently suffered life-threatening complications; one author reported that 30 percent of MAS babies on ventilator support suffered "alveolar rupture." Alveolar meant "relating to the air cells of the lungs"—hole in the lung.

"Mm hmm, lung rupture," Fred said. "Hasn't had that yet."

Babies with MAS had probably suffered from asphyxia before birth and so might also suffer from seizures, coagulopathies, renal failure, and myocardial dysfunction. We pulled out the dictionary and *The Merck Manual.* She hadn't had any seizures. "Coagulopathy has to do with protein in the blood, and clotting," I said.

"Renal failure is kidneys," Fred said.

"Myocardial is heart." This was difficult reading, both intellectually and emotionally; there were so many words to figure out the meanings of, and so many implications attached to the meanings.

Persistent pulmonary hypertension was "increased pulmonary vascular resistance." Pulmonary meaning relating to lungs, vascular meaning relating to a channel for the conveyance of a body fluid (as in blood of an animal or sap of a plant). I'd done an illustrated report on the vascular systems of plants in the fourth grade. I knew these words, but didn't know them all of a sudden, or I wanted to make sure I knew them precisely. Just as the neonatologist had explained, the vessels in her lungs were closed up.

Fred said, "This one mentions the possibility of chronic lung disease." He read from the page: "Long-term abnormalities associated with asphyxia, seizure disorder, psychomotor retardation, are not rare."

"This one says chronic lung disease, neurologic sequelae, pneumothorax. I can't think anymore." I ate a cookie. I assumed "sequelae" involved sequel, following, consequence. I knew the other terms. There were consequences to the trauma of inhaling meconium, and there were consequences to the cure. "Long-term complications should not be neglected. There are few data on the effect of meconium aspiration at birth."

The words in the treatment sections were like landmarks to me: familiar now, after three days of hearing and saying them, but not in themselves entirely known. Full ventilator support. Pavulon to induce paralysis and prevent fighting the ventilator. Rapid rate of ventilation, 60 to 80 breaths per minute. High pressure. Laboratory evaluation including a complete blood count, platelet count, chest X-ray. Arterial blood gases. Echocardiogram to rule out congenital heart disease; they'd done that, too. Intervention was "aimed at using various maneuvers to increase pulmonary blood flow." Maneuvers seemed like just the right word, connoting attempt, capturing the uncertainty with which different moves were tried. Raise this level, lower that one, and see how she does. The guidelines for ventilator treatment of infants with severe MAS were not well established.

"This one calls air leak, or lung rupture, common and an acute emergency," Fred said.

"The nurse called it a setback." I read aloud: "'The infant must be observed for gastrointestinal bleeding, pulmonary hemorrhage, and/or systemic hypotension.' What's hypotension?"

"Blood pressure loss."

"Then you do volume expansion with albumin, plasma, or blood."

"She had albumin yesterday," Fred said.

"If the blood pressure's still low, consider dopamine."

"She's been on dopamine for two days."

"They're doing everything described here," I said, skimming a page. "Antibiotic therapy for bacterial pneumonia, too."

One article concluded that although mechanical ventilation was life saving for many infants, high airway pressures could aggravate the brain swelling and lack of oxygen produced by the initial hypoxic insult. "Insult" seemed appropriate. She inhaled this nasty stuff and then she couldn't breathe. Shit. I could hardly think it, hardly say it. Susan Sontag writes that "A disease of the lungs is, metaphorically, a disease of the soul." Though the upper, more etherealized parts of the body were involved, meconium aspiration originated in "parts of the body (colon, bladder, rectum, breast, cervix, prostate, testicles) that are embarrassing to acknowledge." Not that it mattered, but I did feel a tint of shame when I had to define meconium, just as I felt ashamed that my request for pain relief had begun the chain of events. My body had failed, and I was tainted by the details. What happened to your baby? She breathed in shit.

There were experimental treatments for persistent pulmonary hypertension, with only short-term results known. One treatment involved letting $PaCO_2$—arterial carbon dioxide pressure—rise to a higher level. I didn't understand much of that. Other new treatments included the ECMO, which might improve survival. I pushed the articles away. Food containers, books and papers, and an extra lamp cluttered the table. We both yawned at the mess.

"I'll do this," Fred said. "Why don't you get set up, and I'll bring in the breast pump."

I shuffled down the hall to the bathroom, passing the open nursery door. Fred's closet was in there, and our computer, so we used the room every day. Yellow street light, and the glowing boxes of UCSF Hospital, left the pattern of the venetian blind slats on the dark floor. I was too tired to wish our baby was in there, thinking only of the actual present.

Fred called the ICN before we went to bed and talked with Leeanne. She'd been Cade's nurse the night before, too. "She's worse than earlier, but better than the other night."

"I like Leeanne," I said. "She gives it to you straight."

"None of this 'your baby's turning the corner,'" Fred said. "She's on tomorrow night, too." There were three nursing shifts, with change of shift occurring at 6:45–7:30 a.m., 3–3:45 p.m., and 11–11:45 p.m. We couldn't be in the nursery during these times. We didn't call during change of shift, and we refrained from asking questions just before or after, since the nurse was busy updating or reviewing Cade's chart. The nursing shifts were beginning to order our days. We left the hospital more easily, and slept better, when we liked the nurse who was watching our baby.

When we awoke on Saturday morning, Fred called Leeanne. Cade was the same, a relief to us. She'd experienced desats, or lowered rates of oxygen saturation, throughout the night, but nothing life-threatening. Eventually, the morphine worked to make her comfortable enough to absorb more oxygen.

We did our morning routine. Fred sterilized the breast pump parts by boiling them for five minutes. He filled a large saucepan with water, and had developed a system for placing the funnels, tubes, cups, and filters in the pot so they would all fit. From the bedroom, I could hear him stir the pieces, the pieces knocking together. After being boiled, the pieces were laid on fresh dish-towels to dry, on the kitchen table, which we called the "sterile area." We'd used the stove only for sterilizing for the past three days. Fred brought me cereal in bed. He assembled the breast pump and brought it in to the bedroom. I sat in an armchair with my feet on a cardboard box. Fred attached the tubing to the electrical part of the pump, which was on the floor next to the chair. After I placed a funnel over each breast, he turned on the machine. I asked, "Is it on minimum?" every time, because if the dial were turned too high, the pumping hurt. It hurt a little bit, anyway, as my nipples were pulled out in a regular rhythm by the suction.

The week before I had the baby, our friend Ann had sent a box of baby clothes and her manual breast pump, which came with an instruction booklet. The picture of the single breast pump looked strange enough, a plastic contraption clapped over the breast. But I had laughed out loud at the photograph of a woman using the double pump. She sat erectly in an armchair holding a translucent plastic cone over each breast, a collection cup at-tached to each cone, and tubing leading from each cone to a blue box at her feet. Everything else about the picture was ordinary—the chair, a window with the blind pulled down, blue carpeting, the woman's blond hair parted in the middle and curling up at her shoulders. What was she doing?

Now I sat here, not erectly but hunched over forward so the milk would flow into the cup instead of leaking out the lip of the funnel. Maybe my breasts were the wrong shape, but I didn't think so. When my milk had come in Thursday, my breasts were huge and pointy, cone-shaped. On the telephone I'd said, "Denise, I have movie-star breasts." But I had to tilt forward anyway. I watched TV for fifteen minutes. Fred rushed around cleaning up the bedroom and kitchen, getting dressed, making phone calls. When the time was up, he turned off the pump and eyed the collection cups. "Good amount," he said, like a coach. Every time I used the pump, the amount of milk increased slightly. I had to be sure to drink at least eight glasses of water a day. Fred detached the pump tubing, and carried the whole apparatus into the kitchen, where he poured the milk into a sterile jar, labeled it, and dropped it into the cooler on top of an ice-filled glove. He took apart the equipment, rinsed it, and dropped it in a dishpan of soapy water. Meanwhile I got dressed, still moving a bit slowly. We tried to get to the hospital by eight, most anxious at the morning visit since we hadn't seen Cade for so long.

We were lucky to live only a five-minute drive from Bismarck. Most parents with babies in the ICN lived farther away, since sick newborns from all Bay Area Bismarck hospitals were sent to the San Francisco facility. Some parents had a two-hour drive. We could drive back and forth to the hospital all day, every day, coming home for meals and showers, breast pumping, phone calls. Some parents had premature babies who'd been in the nursery for weeks or months. They drove long distances, and juggled hospital visits with work schedules. We were fortunate to have flexible employment. Fred had planned to take a month off from his part-time fund development job when the baby came, and when she arrived he requested an immediate leave of absence. We made ourselves temporarily unavailable for freelance work, and were thankful that teaching didn't start for another month. We had become parents of one of the 250,000 babies admitted to neonatal intensive care units in the United States each year.

The nursery on Saturday morning was busier with visitors than it had been during the week. As we sat with Cade, we could see mothers and fathers in the middle nursery room whom we hadn't seen before. A nurse held a rigid, squalling, reddish infant over water, demonstrating a bath. Baby Ashley's mother came in, with

Baby Ashley's father and a grim-faced fat little boy, the brother. We'd heard the mother discussing the boy with Ashley's nurse; they were having trouble with him because all the attention was going to Ashley. They received special permission for him to visit the nursery. Now he would see what all the fuss was about. I was concentrating on watching Cade and talking to the nurse; at the edges of my sight and hearing, the boy seemed to pout, and complain. The father led him out.

It was loud in the nursery. A handwritten "Quiet, please" sign hung over Cade's bed, but it was rarely observed. Doctors, nurses, and respiratory therapists conferred with each other, of course. Monitors all over the nursery beeped and were reset. Visitors talked. Cade was supposed to be disturbed as little as possible, because disturbance altered her oxygenation rate, her blood pressure, her heart rate. Noise bothered her, and movement. That was why her hair had never been washed. She'd only been weighed once before today. Diapers were changed with minimal movement, taped loosely or sometimes left untaped. The catheter in her umbilicus was left in for painless blood drawing. We spoke in low voices.

At nine o'clock, a respiratory therapist reduced the oxygen to 98 percent. They would see if she could hold steady at that setting. Now that Fred and I knew more, the staff seemed willing to tell us more. The nurses kept writing in their notes that we were "asking appropriate questions." We asked about the ECMO, but it seemed like a slightly less probable option today, so we didn't push. We looked at all the monitors, drawing connections between the numbers and the articles we'd read.

Dr. Hanover told us that her echocardiogram had proved normal; as he'd suspected, she had no congenital heart defects. Knowing that he had an excellent reputation made me feel friendlier toward him. He wasn't forthcoming, but Cade was still alive.

He certainly was attentive to her. Surveying the nursery, I became aware that doctors didn't ordinarily watch over the babies day and night. They came through for morning rounds and otherwise were available but not necessarily present. Hanover was often by Cade's bed when we came in—he'd be leaning back against the sink, with his arms crossed, watching her. He didn't like to answer questions, but of course we had to ask them. Fred said, "We were wondering about the possibility of brain damage due to lack of oxygen."

"It's a possibility."

"But nothing to think about now, right?" I said lightly. He scratched his head, suddenly distant, serious. He said something technically obscure to us, about the detectability of cranial edema. I guessed I'd made fun of him. I told him four grandparents were coming this weekend.

"Do they live in town?" he asked.

"All from the East Coast."

"Hhmmm." He widened his eyes.

"First grandchild on my side," I said.

"Must be hard," he said.

Nonmedical conversations seemed easier. I looked at Cade. She was yellow—her chest and stomach were pale yellow, not golden-tinged, not pale, or sallow, but wholly yellow. "She's yellow," I said.

Fred peered at her. "She's yellow."

"We may put bilirubin lights on her today," Hanover said. But we were talking around things, jaundice was hardly her problem. It was difficult to remember how her face appeared unswollen. My father would see her soon, and she didn't look like herself.

Dr. Hanover said they'd be starting her transfusion in a minute. I'd forgotten she needed a transfusion. I couldn't give blood so soon after childbirth, and Fred didn't know his type, so they'd used the blood bank. The transfusion would take three hours. I supposed I should be concerned—the risk of tainted blood, or her body reacting against blood that wasn't her own—but a transfusion sounded routine after everything else.

The staff was assembling in the middle nursery room for rounds. "Bye sweetie," I said to Cade. "We'll be back with Grand-dad."

We were sitting in a parents' room when Alan's friend, the woman, came in to retrieve a sweater. She was taking her baby boy home that day.

"How wonderful," I said.

"Yes, his surgery went well. And your baby?"

"She aspirated meconium," Fred said. "She's still critical."

"You know, my baby couldn't aspirate meconium," she said, smiling. "Because he couldn't make any. Incomplete colon." The three of us laughed a little. She looked almost serene, or exhausted. She said goodbye and crossed the hall to the nursery. Somehow we knew—possibly she'd told us—that her family was upset about the Down's Syndrome. Or maybe I assumed they were. I was impressed with how happy she seemed about taking her baby home, and then I thought, *That's old thinking*. Old thinking is that you're terribly sad about a less than perfect baby. It's a shame, and nobody sends flowers. I knew better now. My baby was sick, but still, I was happy when people congratulated me, happy when my mother sent flowers. This woman was happy, too.

Everybody kept telling me on the telephone how brave I was, how well I was handling this. The word "brave" irritated me, and I didn't know what to say in response—Thank you? Yes, we are brave? Maybe Cade was brave, or baby Ashley. We weren't unusual. The ICN on Saturday was full of parents, all of whom had a routine, times they came in, people they telephoned. Everyone around us was doing what we were doing. One mother brought her knitting. A couple sat in low chairs facing an isolette, talking easily to each other, as if they were sitting in the backyard on a summer day. The concept of "brave" seemed wrong.

Still, when I looked at this new mother, I thought, *Now* she's *brave, she's got lonely, difficult times ahead.* I couldn't imagine, or could only partially imagine, being in her situation. With a Down's Syndrome baby, I imagined that one would feel like hiding the baby away. How difficult it would be to push that baby around in a stroller. But one would resist the temptation to be ashamed, and bravely take the baby out in public. Looking at this woman, though, thinking about her later, that whole scheme made no sense. She didn't seem to be resisting anything; she wasn't bucking herself up, holding herself together. She just looked tired, and happy to be taking her baby home.

My father and Maureen came around a corner. We all hugged each other. They appeared refreshingly like civilians—they wore no blue or green scrubs, no white coats, no yellow paper gowns. My father wore khakis, elegant loafers, a crisp shirt, a sweater tied around his neck. Maureen's hair was styled in a flattering new blunt cut.

As a first-time visitor to the ICN, my father had to wash his hands with red liquid soap for five minutes; on subsequent visits it was one minute. I pointed out Cade through the window. He talked about his doctor friend Dudley Hawkes, how he'd had to scrub with a rough charcoal soap in the old days. The liquid soap was nice, he said. I helped him into a gown, which looked funny on him because he was so tall. A puffy yellow minidress. He followed me through the doorway and stood over Cade. He said, "Oh," softly. He touched her a lot, stroking her arm with a fingertip, and I was uncomfortable because we didn't touch her that much, for fear of disturbing her, though maybe touching her was therapeutic. I pointed out the photograph, the puppy, the music box. With the nurse's help, I explained the monitors and equipment arrayed around Cade's bed, as we traced each needle from her skin to its source. She had an IV in each hand, and one on top of her head, one on a foot. These were lines for glucose, dopamine, antibiotics, and the subcutaneous oxygen monitor. The ventilator tube in her mouth. The clear tubing curling out of her bellybutton. Sensors taped to her chest that ran to the heart and blood pressure monitor.

Even after my reading and the hours at Cade's bedside, I couldn't explain everything coherently. In the medical records, the doctors' daily notes are organized into categories such as "I" for IVs, "lytes" for electrolytes, "resp" for respiratory status, and "meds." There was jaundice to consider, and the oxygen index, and the blood count, as well as her weight, breath sounds, and the secretions in the ventilator tube. Today the secretions were a pale yellow mucous. Dad was quiet. His eyes teared a bit. He said how beautiful she was.

Dr. Hanover came in and I introduced them, pleased they should meet. They were similar, in being patriarchal, professionally successful, and prone, when offended, to retreating from friendliness into an intellectual distance. I hoped Hanover would be aware that I came from a respectable family, that my father was well educated. Why did I care that my father was handsome, that he dressed well? Of course, there was a reason to care about class and appearance: Dr. Hanover was comfortable with my father. They both stood and leaned back against the sink with their arms crossed. My father nodded knowingly while Hanover explained that all they could do was try to keep her oxygenated and see if the constricted blood vessels would open. Dr. Hanover said, "If it proceeds in textbook fashion, we should see a change any time now."

"If it goes textbook," my father said, "the situation will just reverse itself."

"Exactly right," Hanover said.

I showed Dad where to discard his gown. Maureen protested a bit that she shouldn't go into the nursery, but we insisted that she should. I felt sorry for Fred, who would accompany her, because Maureen invariably made cutting comments, even when she was trying to be nice. She didn't think much of us. Why are you writers, she'd once questioned us mockingly over cocktails, Do you really think you have something to say? What's your message for the world? Dad and I watched TV in a parents' room, and he put on his professorial reading glasses and skimmed the articles. He would take them to the hotel. He told me he'd asked the congregation of Trinity Episcopal to pray for Cade the next morning. I thought nothing of prayer then, and thanked him, wondering if that was the proper response.

Fred and I went in to say goodbye before the afternoon change of shift. Over the next days, we always went in together after a grandparent departed, to reclaim her, to reclaim each other. "How was it," I asked.

"Fine." His shoulders were tight, his face pale.

The nurse finished her notes for the day. The blood transfusion had been completed, with the baby showing no adverse reaction. She'd secured the breathing tube, given meds, checked the IV sites, taken and recorded a final blood gas for her shift, and put Hypotears in the baby's eyes. She'd talked with us; we seemed to understand the information we'd been given, and were now less anxious, but still appropriately concerned. When I read these notes later, I decided that we must have attained a psychologically desirable state of fear tempered by exhaustion.

We left the hospital through the new wing, decorated in mauve and gray, peaceful, deserted. The gift shop had hardly any gifts in it yet, just a few stuffed animals, a small selection of magazines. On our way out, we saw Alan's friends with their baby in a carrier seat. We couldn't see the baby, and I felt awkward because I wanted to see the baby, the same way people want to see any new baby, but did I especially want to see this one because he was different?

"Congratulations," we said. "And good luck."

"Good luck to you," the woman said. They passed through the automatic glass doors ahead of us and we walked slowly behind them, me taking small old-woman steps. When I thought of them as brave, it seemed like a patronizing thought, because it removed me from them, separated me. They were brave with their problem, while I stood safely where I was. They were victims of circumstance and yet, as victims, I conceived of them as partially to blame for their problem. They had a Down's Syndrome baby because of a genetic flaw, or because they had waited too long to have a child. They were brave with that baby, and I was safely genetically superior, or younger. In the same way, I had my problem baby, a victim, and I was partially to blame for my troubles. We should have stayed on the more expensive insurance plan we'd had at the beginning of my pregnancy, by which my baby would have been delivered by a midwife instead of a doctor, and at UCSF, a nationally renowned hospital. I shouldn't have asked for pain relief during labor, I should have asked about a C-section, about suctioning equipment. A victim could always have acted differently and escaped harm.

The people telling me I was brave had the best intentions, and yet they felt safe in being removed from me. They believed, or possibly just wished, that the same thing wouldn't happen to them. Thinking someone was brave created a gap. I was unable to imagine being that woman carrying her baby out of the hospital. Her damaged baby. Poor thing. How brave. Even though I had a damaged baby upstairs. When people called me brave I said, awkwardly, You'd do the same in my situation. I felt that they truly *were* in my situation, living with whatever flaw or crisis life had presented them with. Whatever they loved, too, could be gone in an hour.

A friend experienced a brutal miscarriage, and when it was over I told her she was brave. I meant it as a compliment, because I admired her strength, her ability to go to work every day for the three weeks while she was bleeding, to cope with pain and uncertainty and disappointment. She was an actor, in a play at the time, and it seemed unbearable that she had to go onstage every night and perform. I said she was brave because I didn't know what else to say. Afterwards, I felt ashamed.

When I entered the nursery that evening, my father was restless. He was prowling around, peering into Ashley's incubator, strolling into the middle nursery room, where three or four members of a family sat around an isolette. My father, an ex-Navy man, enjoyed flirting with rules. He'd ushered us confidently into Princeton reunion tents where we didn't belong for a free roast beef dinner, ordered food for us at a restaurant in Nice when he had no money. He adopted the accent of any state or country, and made himself part of the place. He struck up a conversation with the family in the middle room and stayed in there a few minutes. He came back to Cade but didn't want to sit down. He leaned against the sink, like Hanover.

A therapist I hadn't met, Becca Troy, came in to check Cade's vent settings. She wore pale blue scrubs, but everything else about her was ornamented—her long hair in cornrows with beading at the bottom, dangly gold earrings, red lipstick, long red fingernails. She placed the pads of her fingertips on a tube as if it were a flute, not letting the shiny nails touch it.

Fred and I had met only one respiratory therapist outside a hospital, a man who had approached us in Guatemala to find out when the bus to Solola would come by. We all stood in the shade beside the one paved road. There was no bus station or stop, no posted schedule. "Any minute," I said. He was trying to get to Nebaj, a remote mountain town, a place the army didn't want people visiting, because they'd killed so many people there. We lived lower down, in Panajachel, a heavily touristed town on Lake Atitlan. "Think you'll get there today?" Fred asked him.

He squinted at the late morning sky. "Maybe," he said uncertainly. "Or not. I don't know what I'm doing."

"Why are you going?" I said.

"To see," he said. "I'm an old revolutionary type. Chicago, 1960's, underground. You ever see 'Missing'?"

"Sure," Fred said.

"You know that Frank Terucci character?"

"Journalist," Fred said. "Killed at the stadium."

"We worked together. I still have his toaster oven."

"You have Frank Terucci's toaster oven?" I said.

"Silverware, too. Before he left for Chile, he had a garage sale." He unzipped his windbreaker. "Maybe I shouldn't go up there."

"What do you do now?" I said.

"I'm a respiratory therapist in Boston." It didn't strike me one way or another, except he didn't appear to make much money. He wore cheap lace-up shoes, carried a vinyl shoulderbag. "I like helping people breathe," he said. The old schoolbus came rocketing down the long curving hill into town, its roof piled high with luggage and market baskets, a man leaning out of the door crying, "Solola."

"Are you going?" I said.

The man sighed.

"To Solola, then to Los Encuentros," Fred said. "Then you'd better ask someone."

"I'm going," the man said resolutely. We waved at the bus,

which creaked and jounced to a stop, and he squeezed his way inside.

"Solola?" the driver's assistant said.

"Nebaj," the man said, and the assistant shook his head discouragingly.

We called, "Good luck!" He waved from the crowded aisle. I thought of respiratory therapy as a vocational calling because of him. What could be more essential than breath?

"Looks a little better tonight," Becca said.

My father said that Becca had been telling him and Fred earlier that Cade's meconium aspiration was a total surprise. The respiratory team was not on standby status, as they are when any problem is anticipated. I'd heard announcements over the speaker system in the nursery for standby. It might be "Stand by, labor room two," and the respiratory therapist would pick up equipment resembling a hard-sided suitcase, and several people would run down the hall for labor and delivery.

"You weren't on standby for this one?" I asked.

"No." She shook her head adamantly. "We got called after, and we tried to set up as fast as we could." She looked me in the eye. "Total surprise." She spied something on a shelf. "There's that vibrator," she said, pocketing it. It was luna-moth green, as if it glowed in the dark.

"We use that to stimulate the chest," she said, laughing because I was staring at her.

My father shook his head. "You'd never think of that," he said, and we all laughed, letting sex into the room for a moment, like a vapor to sustain us.

5

Becca Troy had taken charge when Cade was first admitted to the intensive care nursery. She'd ordered around a team of people, saying I need this, I want that. Fred had assumed she was a doctor.

"So she wasn't in labor and delivery?" I asked. We were sitting in a parents' room with my father and Maureen.

"No," he said. "While the nurse was suctioning the baby, a lot of people came in to the triage room, but no respiratory therapists, no one from the ICN."

"They hadn't been called yet?" I said.

"I don't know. They must have thought the baby was all right, because they had me cut the cord."

"It was already cut," I said.

"Of course it was cut," he said sharply, then lowered his voice. "And clamped. But it had to be shortened, so they asked me."

"The ceremonial thing," I said. They'd had him perform this ritual gesture in a triage room, after they'd suctioned out meconium, while she took breath after damaging breath. "Didn't they know she was sick?"

"They didn't know," he whispered defensively. "I'm just telling you what happened." Maureen, Fred and I sat squeezed onto the undersized tweed couch.

"My god," Maureen said.

My father, the tallest, sat sunk in the squishy chair, his fingers laced together. "When did they manage to figure it out?" he said.

"I don't know," Fred said. "They told me to go on back and wait with Kathryn, and they'd bring her to the labor room."

"You told me they'd bring her in a few minutes," I said.

"But no one came in."

How had Fred acted when he came back to the labor room? I'd been tiredly cleaning the blood off my right hand, the meconium off my left. Here's some juice, I'd said to him. I'd seen the baby fleetingly. I had the image of her face, a sense of her size and weight on my belly, but then she was carried away—it happened instantly, without sound or logic, like a dream.

"I got worried," he said. "I went back to the triage room to see, but the room was empty. I looked around and saw a sign for intensive care, went there, and saw all this activity through the window and assumed it was our baby."

"No one told you?" Maureen said, and my father shook his head slowly, back and forth.

He shrugged. "Everyone was rushing around. Becca was pointing and shouting, 'I want that tube cut to five,' numbers and directions. Someone saw me and said, 'The father's here.' Then Hanover came out."

We'd been through labor together, and delivery, and then I lay in bed in a closed room, trying to eat, get cleaned up, go to the bathroom. Fred watched the nurse bring up meconium, and walked the halls, coming upon an emergency scene for his baby.

And for Cade, every breath burned her lungs and people bent close to her face to shove tubes down her trachea, down her esophagus. Fred and I could try to twine our two stories together to make one. She was still alone.

"You called me before you went and found her in intensive care," my father said.

"Yes, and I told you she'd had trouble breathing but was okay. That's how it was presented to me. I didn't have a good feeling, though."

I'd made him call the grandparents, knowing they were anxious for news. I kept thinking of our friends' baby, how she had aspirated meconium, and the pediatricians had whisked her away to work on her. How scary that must have been, I'd said. Yes, but they had brought her back a few minutes later, breathing well. Their hospital was better prepared for meconium, maybe because the baby was overdue, and overdue babies are especially at risk for meconium.

My father leaned forward. "The deal is that if they'd noticed the problem and suctioned out this stuff immediately, she wouldn't be hooked up to a respirator now?"

"That's the deal," Fred said.

"I've seen bad hospitals before," Maureen said. "But this—" She gave a low laugh. We always laughed, clipped short laughs, laughs of disbelief, sarcastic laughs. Our anger was never pure. It was mixed with self-consciousness, an awareness that our situation was terrible yet common, that countless people had lost a child, had stood in a hospital hallway wanting to scream at a doctor. Our child wasn't even dead—how angry could we be?

We sat with Cade for a while after Dad and Maureen left. She lay on her back with her head turned to one side. The nurses turned her head several times a day. Fred and I alternated sitting on the side she was facing. Tonight he faced her. When I looked at her closed eyes, her nose and open mouth, I felt intimate with her, as if we could exchange energy by facing each other. When I looked at the back of her head, I was liable to check the monitors more often, talk with the nurse. Her blood pressure still dipped too low whenever she was handled. To decrease her pain and keep her still, she was given morphine and pavulon almost every two hours. She was maintaining good oxygenation with a lower concentration of oxygen, 89 percent, and her dopamine dosage was being gradually lowered, too. It was Saturday, and she hadn't experienced a near-death crisis since Thursday morning. We said goodnight to her, gently stroking her arms and her hair with our fingertips.

Fred slung my canvas bag over his shoulder. "How do you feel?" he said.

"It's tiring to be angry."

He kept his arm around me as we walked the long hallways. At night, visitors had to leave through the old wing and go out the emergency room entrance. Security guards patrolled the hospital halls at night, and gave clip-on visitor passes to people who were allowed to be there. As parents of a baby in the ICN, we could be at the hospital at any time. If we arrived after seven, we signed in at the emergency room entrance after the guard called the ICN and got authorization for us. When we left we signed out. Was the heavy nighttime security for people or medical equipment? It seemed odd that there was so little security during the day. Guards did sit at desks at the hospital entrances and opposite the elevators on the maternity floor, but no one signed in or wore visitor badges. The only baby ever kidnapped at a Bay Area hospital had been taken two months before, from Alta Bates hospital in the middle of the day by a woman who posed as a social worker. The sixteen-year-old mother handed Baby Kerri to the woman, hours after the baby's birth, and the woman had simply walked out of the hospital.

I had read the newspaper accounts of it as I waited for the bus to go to the obstetrician. People interviewed expressed horror about the kidnapping, but there was also an undercurrent of reproach toward the mother. She was too young to have a baby. She shouldn't have given the baby to a stranger. On television the mother cried and said she had the crib all ready, the toys waiting. As if to defend her love for the baby to those who might have been thinking, Did she really *want* that baby? So young, not married, the gangly pale boyfriend-father hovering near her, touching her arm, but she didn't want to be touched; she was crying on her makeup, hunching forward in her shapeless T-shirt. The cameras stayed right on her, and the lights threw the living room around her into shadow and made it look shabby and brown. Cry if you love your baby, cry for the shame of having handed her over. Several months later, Baby Kerri was found, her kidnapper turned in by a neighbor. Security was tight at hospitals now, and new mothers were warned not to give their baby to anyone, except a familiar nurse.

The nighttime security at Bismarck, though, seemed designed as much to protect the hospital as the people in it. A whole new shell was being built over the old hospital, which made the interior labyrinthine and unpredictable; one day we'd take a certain elevator, and the next day it would be gone, concealed behind a seamed wall of sheetrock. Within days, labor and delivery was scheduled to be moved to a new unit, with windows in the labor rooms, rocking chairs, and jacuzzi tubs in the private bathrooms. While I was pregnant, we'd joked that if the baby were overdue, my consolation prize would be a brand new luxury labor room. The intensive care nursery would disappear, too, transplanted to a larger space, but we didn't joke about that. We just noticed the details of the hospital as they shifted, the X-ray lab shut down one day, a bewildered patient squinting at a cardboard sign on the door. It was disconcerting to walk the basement corridor and pass abandoned gurneys and EKG machines. We signed out at emergency and surrendered our badges.

At home, we stayed up until change of shift was completed at 11:45 p.m., then called to check in with the new nurse. Fred talked to Leeanne, who told him that they'd lowered Cade's oxygen to 85 percent; her sats had dipped, so they'd raised the oxygen back up to 92 percent. We couldn't believe she had been weaned down to 85 percent, even for a few minutes. How daring of them, how unexpected for us.

"Eighty-five percent," I said. "I never thought we'd see below ninety."

"They'd better be careful," Fred said.

"I know." But we were happy. We watched television. We had a Polaroid of Cade on top of the TV. We'd tried to take pictures but our camera broke in the act, so a nurse had gotten an instant camera out of the big cabinet and stood on a chair and snapped two shots looking down at Cade on her bed. We put one in an acrylic frame and there was our little girl, eyes closed, her mouth obscured by tape and tubing, our sweet little baby. Late at night we relaxed more. The East Coast was long asleep; no one would call, unless the hospital did. We got into bed and watched "David Letterman." My mind was pleasantly blank. Fred furiously flossed his teeth. "What's up?" I said.

"Incompetents," he said, deep into an angry thought.

"I know."

When I called Leeanne at 5:15 a.m., the baby's oxygen was still at 92 percent. "How's her sat rate?"

"Low nineties. What we expect," said Leeanne. Her sat rate

had been in the high nineties before. Maybe, we concluded, they were happy with a lower rate during the weaning process.

In the morning, my mother arrived at our apartment before we went to the hospital. Like Dad, she'd had a difficult trip; the only flight she could get on was for San Jose, so she'd rented a car and driven up late the previous night. I showed her the picture of Cade, and she smiled the crooked way she does when she's about to cry, gave a big sniffle, and said, "Oh honey, she's beautiful." She put her arm around me and looked at the messy apartment. On the bamboo thing that passed for a couch were piled carefully separated stacks of extra breastpump equipment from Ann, a variety of jackets, mail, shoes, and trash. My hospital bag, rifled through but still packed, sat on the floor, surrounded by some of its contents. Mom said cheerfully, "Shall I make coffee?" She'd always swooped in, wherever I lived, and done whatever needed doing to make daily life feel not only possible, but pleasing. She'd arrive with a new sweater or novel for me, buy tulips, hang curtains. Why had I hesitated to have her come?

An unfamiliar nurse sat at the head of Cade's bed and looked at us over the rim of her reading glasses. She was older than any nurse we'd had. We hadn't known the nurse for Saturday either; we figured the usual nurses had the weekend off. This nurse didn't say much to us. Cade's oxygen percentage was down to 72. We leaned toward the monitor. "That says 72?" I said.

"It sure does," Fred said. "And her sat rate's 97." We sat in silence, looking at Cade, who appeared exactly the same as the night before, but was somehow surviving on less oxygen. As we watched over her, we saw one of her legs stir.

"Did you see that?" one of us asked the other.

We didn't know. It had happened so quickly. We stared intently at her legs, but she was still. Then a leg twitched and her torso seemed to shudder briefly, smoothing almost instantly into stillness. As on the surface of water, no trace remained of the movement of a moment before.

"I think she moved," I ventured to the nurse, who looked over her glasses.

"I don't think so," she said.

"Maybe the pavulon is wearing off," I said.

The nurse checked the chart. "She's not due for another two hours." She sighed and got up from her chair. She reached over the baby and pinched the flesh of her lower leg hard between a thumb and forefinger. The leg lifted slightly with the force of it and then dropped. "See," the nurse said, turning away. "Nothing."

A few seconds later, the whole leg moved in a slow writhe, trembled, then relaxed. "She moved," I said.

"Oh yes she did," Fred said.

"Well," the nurse shrugged and gave an unfriendly smile. "She'll get more when it's time."

It felt difficult for me to breathe. Maybe one of us suggested more morphine. The doctors were assembling in the anteroom for rounds. We stood up to leave. "We'll be back at one," I said.

"See you folks later." She waved and returned to reading a book.

As we walked down the hall, I whispered angrily, "I hate her. Did you see what she did?"

"She's a bitch," Fred said. "No doubt about it."

"What can we do?"

"Nothing. Complain to the nursing supervisor."

"Do we want to do that?" I asked.

"I don't know." We kept a tense silence as we walked out, past labor room 1, past the labor and delivery staff, the reception nurse, an anxious family in the waiting area, the payphone, the vacant-faced security guard, into the slow elevator, down the long mauve hallway, past the half-stocked giftshop, and out.

"Bitch," I said aloud. "She hurt our baby."

We talked furiously in the car. "Disturbance interferes with her sat rate," I said.

"At least it was rounds," Fred said. "The doctors will check her now."

"How could you pinch a baby like that?"

"I don't know."

"Should we have said something?"

"I don't know."

I wanted to scream. At her. At myself, for being so polite to her. I always smiled and kept quiet, then got angry later when it wouldn't help. Why didn't I say, at least, Please don't do that again. Carol stuck up for her husband in Milwaukee. Betsy stuck up for Jonathan when he was in intensive care. She'd told us that Jonathan's chart included comments about her: "Mother very aggressive, asks too many questions." How could there be too many questions? Cade lay there helpless, silenced, paralyzed. We had to be her advocates. I felt angry at Fred. Why didn't he say something? Passive, just like his father, I thought, knowing he'd hate that. Why were we diplomatic? "Why didn't we say anything to her?" I burst out.

"Look," Fred said. "She's a bitch of a nurse. It's not our fault. We can decide whether to put in a complaint."

"Okay." I tried to calm myself. "It's suffocating, trying to act right."

"They're always watching," Fred said. Of course they were, because it was part of their job. We felt acutely self-conscious from the moment we passed labor and delivery and turned down the hallway to the nursery. We smiled at the social worker, Nina, if we saw her. She always asked about breastpumping, and I was beginning to feel that bringing milk was slightly absurd, that it was more for my sake than Cade's, and I resented her secret strategy for me. Twenty-five little labeled jars of milk now crowded a shelf of the nursery freezer, and I was producing more and more. How could Cade ever drink it all? But when we saw Nina we smiled and said my milk was coming well. We smiled at other parents, at the receptionist. We hesitated to get chairs for ourselves if we had to ask anyone to move out of our way to get them. We jumped up instantly if anyone needed to get to the IV cart or check a monitor. We asked questions, but not, we felt, too many. We apologized if we asked the same question twice, because we'd forgotten or hadn't understood the answer. We left for change of shift and rounds without being asked. All of this was natural courtesy. Cade seemed to be getting good care, and, until this morning, her nurses had been kind and capable. Everyone in the ICN was under stress and we tried not to make it worse. We generally felt friendly toward them, grateful for their knowledge and care, for teaching us about Cade's treatment. But sometimes being nice strained us, as we tried to take up as little space as possible on our stools, to time our questions for when the nurse looked less busy. And clearly I'd become so used to being accommodating, in the nursery, maybe in my whole life, that I didn't know when to speak up. When Fred and I met Dad and Maureen for lunch, I said, childish in my anger, "The nurse today is mean. She pinched the baby."

At Howard's restaurant we all ate eggs. Our usual waitress smiled and poured coffee into thick white cups. Last weekend I'd sat sideways in a chair because of my huge belly; now I sat deflated, pulled up to the table. The waitress asked nothing; maybe she heard us say "hospital" or "intensive care." Dad and Maureen talked about the presidential election. Talking about the nurse only agitated us. Had Cuomo ruined his career by not entering the race? I'd eaten many meals while listening to my parents, grandfather, uncles, sister and cousins debate one issue or another. What did the Russian Revolution accomplish? Did Carter's foreign policy redeem his domestic policy? I don't know the answers to these questions. I'd listen and listen, picking up fragments about the early labor movement, black voter registration in Texas, the legalization of casino gambling in New Jersey. At dinner candles were lit, the grownups drank wine, and everyone stayed at the table for a long time. In 1972 I'd proudly worn a "Love McGovern" t-shirt to school and helped my parents stuff envelopes in campaign offices. For me, the subtext of politics was security, because politics would never end, and this meant more than the text. No matter who got divorced, or moved far away, or even died, the subject would always be there. In the diner, I felt almost tranquilized.

Fred and I went into the nursery first to check on Cade. She slept without moving. Or she didn't sleep. I could hardly bear to think of her as conscious, as experiencing pain and not understanding it. This was her entrance to the world.

Having left my mother with Dad and Maureen, I hurried out of the nursery to check on them, perhaps to smooth the conversation, or fill a disagreeable silence. Though my parents had attended my college graduation and wedding together, I hardly regarded them as friends. Our one attempt at family therapy years before had deteriorated into them arguing over whose fault it was that I had become so disturbed. But as I walked into the parents' room, my mother was saying easily, "Someone had a heart attack on your flight?"

"It was unbelievable," Maureen said.

"Paramedics took him off on a stretcher," my father said.

"So you had to fly to Los Angeles?"

"At midnight," my father said.

"You're kidding."

"Excuse me," I interrupted. "Who's going in first?"

"Teel, you haven't seen her," my father said. "You go first."

"Thank you," my mother said. "I'll just leave my jacket." She took off the houndstooth-check jacket my sister and I coveted, and draped it on the couch. Her blond hair was held back in a tortoise-shell barrette; she wore wide-legged silk pants and a turtleneck sweater, and looked terrific. Why had I been so worried?

I showed Mom how to scrub, and fastened a yellow gown on her. When Fred saw us through the window he came out, so we could visit together.

"Her face is puffy," I said. "From fluids."

"She looks just like you," Mom whispered. I smiled. I knew my mother wanted her to look like me, just as she'd wanted me to have a girl, to replicate her happy experience.

"The nurses think she looks like Fred," I said. I touched Cade's arm and said, "Your grandma Teel is here, honey." I told Mom to touch her arm. I explained the various monitors. Her oxygen was down to 46 percent, which I could hardly believe.

My mother said, "She'll be fine. She's strong, just like her mother." Though Cade had seemingly improved over the past day, I wasn't ready to surrender to optimism. I'd assumed a stiff mental posture, bracing myself for bad news, and wasn't about to relax just yet. When Fred and I read the monitors that day, we gave each other cautious smiles, but said little.

Toward the end of the hour, Dad and Fred sat in the nursery. As I turned into the parents' room, I heard Mom saying to Maureen, "She doesn't want to, but she's going to have to get another catscan." Only two hours before, I'd reminded her that Cecily hadn't yet told Dad about her illness.

"Mom," I hissed. "Stop it. I told you not to talk about that." I glared at her, then turned away, exasperated at the way she'd gossip about us, just to make conversation when she felt awkward with someone. As I turned my head, I saw tears in her eyes. She sat, silenced, on a couch. What a bitch I was, who thought of myself as the diplomat, the one who gracefully prevented conflict.

I remembered those same sudden tears in my sister's eyes when I'd called her a snob for not liking the wine Fred and I drank at home. Her boyfriend had clasped her hand under the table. All the wicked big sister stories she must have told him. I was mean. My mother chewed her finger. After Maureen left the room, I apologized.

"I thought you said Cecily *had* told her father about that," she said.

"No, I said she *hadn't.*"

A new resident, Paul Meegan, strutted around the nursery all afternoon, introducing himself to the parents, chatting up the nurses, conspicuously making notes on a clipboard. He took detailed notes on Cade's vital signs, uric output, appearance, vent settings, breath sounds and medications. If she continued to progress, they would try to lower the oxygen pressure. Dr. Meegan happened to be replacing his wife, Susan Meegan, who started a new rotation the next day. Residents spent 30 days in the ICN.

"I don't start until tomorrow," he said. "But I'm familiarizing myself with all the cases. Looks like your little girl has turned a corner." He patted me on the shoulder, and flashed his teeth. "Textbook case," he said.

When he'd gone, Fred and I rolled our eyes at each other: Paul, perfect resident. He was younger than we were, and he'd better not pat me on the shoulder again, I thought. Cade did seem more stable, though. "We've got the prayer machine working," my Dad had told Becca earlier. "We've got the power of grandparents. Two grandparents in, and two more on the way." A strong baby, a textbook case, medicine, a prayer, a voice—whatever worked was working, maybe. No one mentioned the ECMO now.

At home we all ate an early dinner of our friend Denise's baked chicken, mashed potatoes, and salad. Mom and Dad talked about work—she had just been helicoptered up to headquarters for a company meeting; he had been Lear-jetted to Ohio. As in the child's game of scissors, paper, rock, I wondered: *Did a Lear jet beat a helicopter?*

"What do you think Clinton will do for the pharmaceutical industry?" my father said.

"He talks a good game," my mother said. "As for what he'll do . . ."

"Salad?" Maureen passed the bowl to me.

"Thanks," I said. "Can you believe Denise made all this food?"

"You tell her this chicken is delicious," my mother said.

"Good spuds," my father said.

Fred stood up. "Would anyone like wine?"

"Good idea," my mother said.

"I could have a glass of wine," my father said. "Help me sleep on the plane."

I looked at them sitting across the table from each other and thought, *Wouldn't you guys be perfect together?* Of course they hadn't been nice to each other in their marriage. Ten years before, eight years after their separation, they'd still hated each other passionately. "I hate that man," my mother said one night. "I'd like to punch your mother in the face," my father said one night. Both of them pacing in separate living rooms. I always thought, *Thank God they're divorced, imagine a household with the two of them!* When I was little they would yell at each other in the kitchen, below my bedroom, and I would pound on the bed and shout, "Stop it! Stop it!" But they didn't stop, and then we lived with our mother, and the house was peaceful.

Eventually he married Maureen, but he didn't seem happy. When we visited, Maureen cooked elaborate meals and he drank a tumbler of scotch in the kitchen while she drank a tumbler of vodka. Then they often fought bitterly at the dinner table until one of them stamped wearily up the stairs, head down like an old

horse. Maureen told us that he only became upset when we visited. Cecily and I tried so hard, as we sat at dinner over the years,
to say nothing that would provoke him—nothing about our
mother, nothing about our lives that might smack of self-con-
gratulation, nothing self-deprecating that might be seconded and
developed into a lecture, nothing about him, nothing about
politics, nothing about work, religion, or spending money, nothing about emotionally difficult subjects like the death of a friend—
that we developed the art of conversing pleasantly about precisely
nothing. Still, something might set him off, and Maureen would
needle him. Cecily and I sat next to each other, with our stepsister
across from us. Our eyes met to signal caution, sympathy, amuse-
ment. Once, during a particularly loud uproar, all three of us even
managed to hold hands under the table. There were flickers of
light in our father's life—he went back to the church, he got a
wonderful job—but no metamorphosis. Dad would always be this
way, would always live in this house.

The next time I saw him, two months after this visit with Cade,
my father was living alone in a one-room apartment. He and
Maureen had seen a marriage counselor, but there seemed to be
no love left. He attended AA meetings. At dinner, he drank a
Klausthaler, a non-alcoholic beer. He told me that after we'd all
visited the baby that evening and said goodbye, Maureen hadn't
spoken to him for the whole of the flight home, and the next
day. She was angry at him for the amiable way he had spoken to
my mother—he had flirted with her, she charged, he was still in
love with her. It was another fight in a long string of them, but it
must have been nearly the last one. I understood how difficult it
must have been for my father to fly out that weekend in August
with Maureen and see me and my mother, and sit by the bedside
of his critically ill granddaughter. He was in the midst of a crisis

himself. For some time, Fred and I lived in the tunnel of our baby's illness, knowing little else.

My parents met us at the hospital that evening and shared the visiting hour. Maybe they felt connected in being grandparents together, both there to see their granddaughter, to meet her and possibly say goodbye to her. Maybe they felt partly sad that they weren't still married. I didn't think of their tenderness, only their animosity, and tried to be scrupulously fair in portioning out the hour: the most time for my father, since he was leaving soon, then for my mother, and the least for Maureen, since she was a step-grandmother. Yet I wanted to make sure she felt included, because it seemed that being with Cade could make us feel like one family.

My father touched Cade's arm with his finger and told her how strong she was. He stroked the matted hair on the side of her head, away from the IV needle. We examined her ears together— they didn't seem to stick out, as ours both did. "I know mine stuck out by six months," I said. "Because of that Christmas picture."

"We'll have to wait and see." He gave an exaggerated sigh.

"I'm glad you saw her," I said.

"She'll be all right," he said. "She's a fighter." He whispered goodbye and we left the nursery together. *Would she be all right*, I wondered. And if so, had I been wrong to present the situation in the way I did, causing everyone to fly out here at great expense and inconvenience? If she didn't die, had they wasted their money? We said goodbye in the hall; they were taking a redeye flight back, and had to go to work the next morning.

"Thanks for coming." I hugged my father tightly.

"She'll be all right," he said. "You guys are doing great. Hang in there, Ace." They waved as they turned the corner, back toward labor and delivery, toward the exit. I took a deep breath. I was glad that he came. There was no difference between what was for him, what was for me, and what was for the baby.

In the morning when Fred called, Leeanne was cautious. "Did they reduce the oxygen level further?" he asked. Yes, but they raised it again. I used the breastpump and we dressed quickly and drove to the hospital. Perhaps Dr. Beckman, who'd had night duty for the first time since Cade's birth, had acted too aggressively. Hanover had watched over her for days like a big old hen, and then Beckman got in there and wanted to turn some dials. Hanover the cautious, a big ruddy bearded man, and Beckman the aggressive, a small pale man with glasses. We laughed in the car. Beckman the maniac.

Cade was all right. We hadn't expected progress. Her oxygen was at 50 percent. They would wait a while and then try to reduce the oxygen again. We felt excited that her oxygen had been reduced so far from 100 percent; we'd become accustomed to her being on pure oxygen, forced in at high pressure, at a rapid breath rate, as if these conditions provided a safe resting place for her. She was stable, and hadn't needed the lung bypass machine. The respirator and the medications worked together to oxygenate her blood at a satisfactory rate. Oxygen flowed through her body to her brain. Her blood pressure held. Yet we were in the doldrums, a stillness that brought no peace. She couldn't stay here, with harsh oxygen being forced into her lungs. Her lungs would collapse, or be irremediably damaged.

On this Monday morning, her seventh day of life, her urine output was too low, her bladder distended. Because of the pavulon, Cade did not pee on her own. A nurse would massage her bladder and she would urinate. But the bladder massage wasn't working anymore. Dr. Meegan ordered a catheter set up. Her heart rate dipped so low that the nurse filled out a heart rate report sheet for the first time, twice. Copious mucous secretions were suctioned out, since the tube irritated the baby's respiratory tract. Everyone was waiting for her, as they said, to "turn the corner." First they'd had to get oxygen into her blood, and now they had to wean her down from pure oxygen to 20 percent oxygen, or room air. Dr. Hanover and Dr. Meegan seemed restless. They would step in, glance at the baby, and step out to confer in the anteroom. I felt protective of Cade, like they were trying to push her too fast. *Let her be,* I thought, feeling edgy as they paced around.

"We'll try a tiny bit at a time," Jim, the respiratory therapist, said. "Very gradual. If she doesn't respond, we'll turn it back up."

We didn't discuss the risks of prolonged treatment with the medical team; they had taught us that looking to the future was inappropriate at this point. When we talked to people on the telephone they often asked, "How long?"

"If everything goes well, a few weeks, at best," we said, making it up. The articles we'd read focused on treatment and said little about associated risks. We'd been watching the nurses, doctors, and respiratory therapists attend to her oxygen, heart rate, blood pressure, pH levels, body fluids, and pneumonitis, trying to keep her alive while causing the least possible damage. For the first few days, we concentrated on her being alive. As she experienced more hours of stability, and the team discussed weaning her from pure oxygen, we thought of damage, too. If she lived, what condition would she be in? I sat by her and touched her arm and talked to her, wishing for her to pull through. If she suffered lasting harm, we'd deal with it in its own time. We hoped for her strength, and for a stability that would allow her blood vessels to relax out of their trauma-induced constriction. *Let the air flow through,* I'd think as I stared at her closed eyes, her chest rising and falling according to the ventilator setting.

The night before, while my mother read the medical articles

for the first time, we'd reread the sections on potential damage. One study found that 3 out of 14 infants on respirators for more than 24 hours suffered from upper airway obstruction after the tube was removed, and one of these required prolonged tracheostomy. We were startled that the field of study was so small. Fourteen infants? The other articles didn't give numbers, but we suddenly realized the rarity of full-blown meconium aspiration syndrome. And how many infants with MAS progressed to persistent pulmonary hypertension? When the authors of these articles mentioned death, brain swelling, brain damage, hole in the lung, chronic lung disease, kidney failure, how many babies had they studied? On how many babies were the treatment guidelines based?

In the nursery, when Dr. Hanover stepped in and leaned against the sink for the sixth or seventh time in an hour, Fred asked, "How rare is meconium aspiration syndrome?"

He thought for a few moments. "I see about 3 a year."

On our labor and delivery tour, the nurse had told us that 150 babies were delivered every month at Bismarck; that meant 1800 a year. Three out of 1800, or 1 out of 600. Our baby was 1 out of 600. Since critically ill babies from other Bay Area Bismarck hospitals were sent to the San Francisco intensive care nursery, and babies from non-Bismarck hospitals were referred to Dr. Hanover, the chances were even less than 1 in 600 that a baby born at San Francisco Bismarck would have meconium aspiration syndrome. I sat on the stool, watching Cade and thinking, *Did my blood pressure drop cause it? Why had I asked for pain relief? Why wasn't I stronger?* Forty percent of women who delivered at Bismarck received epidural anesthesia—why did I react badly to it? Did they give me too much? Was I a weak person? I wanted to ask Hanover what happened to the other babies he'd seen who had meconium aspiration, but I didn't. What would be the point? If they had died, knowing wouldn't help me. If they had lived, it didn't mean my baby would live. Statistics couldn't comfort me, when my baby had a one-sixth of one percent chance of MAS, and here she lay, the sickest baby in the nursery.

Sometimes I would think "sickest baby in the nursery," which filled me with dread, and a righteous anger at Dr. Greg, and then I would drop the phrase from my mind and return to the present. How was her blood gas, I would ask the nurse. See you after rounds, Fred would say.

At home my mother set the table with cloth napkins and tall glasses of mineral water. Our friend Alan had brought more food, and she served plates of sesame noodles and salad. "Sit down and eat, honey," she said. She'd actually bought a new broom and swept the kitchen. Clean laundry was stacked on a chair. She'd made our apartment into a civilized, welcoming place. My mother, along with our other relatives and friends, steadily connected us to a reality outside the hospital and supported us. Accustomed to independence, we felt surprised and grateful.

I called the director of medical affairs at my mother's company, whom we hadn't spoken to over the weekend. We discussed the baby's progress, and then I said, "We've been reading about meconium aspiration, and it seems to be largely preventable. Is it true that delivery rooms should be equipped for aspiration, intubation, and oxygenation?"

"Having aspirating equipment at bedside is what they were doing twenty-five years ago," he said, "when I was a Bismarck pediatrician. It's not rocket science."

We returned to the hospital and entered the nursery anteroom after rounds on Monday, just as Dr. Greg and Dr. Royce passed Cade's bed and walked into the center room. I saw them through the window as I put on a yellow gown, and they seemed hardly to stop by Cade—they glanced down at her and kept moving. Or maybe they had been standing over her for a while before we arrived. I studied them through the anteroom window. Their heads were alike, curving out in back, tapering to the fine necks, apparent because of their short hair. Dr. Greg was dark-skinned, with straightened hair, and a flash of gold somewhere— a wristwatch? Dr. Royce had carrot-colored hair. They wore blue scrubs and their heads, their fine noses leading, moved in tandem. They caught my stare and half smiled and kept walking.

"Get out," Fred said to himself.

"I can't stand them," I whispered. Why had they come? To see what Greg had done? Did she think she'd made a mistake? Did she accept responsibility? She wouldn't admit wrongdoing, be-cause of legal implications, but did she feel remorse? Next time she delivered a baby, would she say, What do I do now, or would she examine it more closely? The way Dr. Royce instructed her on how to stitch me up made me wonder if Greg had just been hired. The two of them had stared at me when I said it hurt, as if I'd been rude to interrupt them; they'd given me an injection in silence, then resumed talking to each other. They seemed in col-lusion, they seemed arrogant. Did they know the baby might die? Had someone told them? Did everyone talk to each other in a hospital? They must. We were hopelessly outside of knowing who said what. Would Greg get in trouble? Would she be protected from blame, or would someone mind the expense of the nursery; Bismarck is a system unto itself, in which doctors are part-owners. I wished someone would give her a hard time. I wished she couldn't glide untouchable through the nursery, behind glass, half smiling.

6

A few years ago, in Italy, I woke up in a hotel room to see my mother's bed empty. My sister still slept. As I dressed, I was pleased to be able to think of clues: she would be out walking, toward the middle of town, on a sunny street. I hailed her five minutes later and she cried out, How did you know where to find me?

Her father has died last year and, while grieving, she feels liberated. As the only daughter of four children, she was given the least respect. Unlike her brothers, she wasn't bankrolled as she pursued a vocation, though she'd always wanted to be an attorney. There was no expense account set up for her at the clubby Monocle Restaurant in Washington, D.C., no political connections passed along, except the one that gave her the job of being a secretary for Lyndon Johnson. She got into college by filling out a friend's extra application, worked as a secretary at Cornell University while my father earned a Ph.D., and finally entered law school at age 35, her daughters then nine and six years old. Her marriage ended in the summer after her first year. I know these things and more, yet if my mother died tomorrow I would touch her belongings with hope, as if they held revelations. I would be bound, on a search for her.

What is the poetry she writes for herself? What is her favorite music, and why does she go to Africa to walk for days through long grass, looking for animals? We trade psychological information, about her alcoholic mother, my alcoholic father. But our passions remain sealed, which may be their preservative. My father presents himself, a complex, coherent package of Navy stories, poems, hopes, obligations, and failures. He talks until late at night. My mother *seems* to present herself, as we drink wine, go out walking, go shopping. But she's distracted—where is she?

My sister and I piece her together subject by subject: she can't tolerate illness because Grandma drank and smoked herself to death, wearing a silky bathrobe all day, watching television. Grandma sent her second baby away because she couldn't care for two children at once. Mildred the housekeeper raised Mom, the first baby, and Mom raised her three brothers. Cecily and I laugh as we recall me lying on the couch with the flu, Mom standing over me saying, "It's all caused by stress. You need to come swimming with me at the Y." She can't stand to see someone fall down, because they might never get up again. She can't stand to be helpless.

In the parents' room at the hospital, we prepared to say goodbye. My mother would take a redeye flight back to Washington. "She'll be fine, honey," she said.

"We'll see." I was annoyed. If she'd be fine, then why was she on a respirator? I'd glided into a natural politeness with my father, deeply appreciative that our relationship seemed to be relaxing out of artifice. I was grateful for his presence and for his encouragement. But my mother and I had suffered no estrangement, and I was used to telling her what I really thought. When *she* said the baby would be fine, I wanted more honesty than that. I wanted her to tolerate the uncertainty of Cade's prognosis with me. But she was leaving now. Up a steep hill banked with flowering trees, I walked her to her rental car and we hugged goodbye. The country she'd fly over, sharp mountains giving way to desert, greening into farmland which would become steadily populated in the East, felt vast to me. I hitched my bag up on my shoulder and climbed into our car, where Fred waited.

I was my mother's first baby. Now I had a baby girl. Cade and I were beginning in a strange way. I'd stare at her and think, *Just live and I'll give you anything you want.* Would I be able to give her myself?

I could pump milk, take a sitz bath, and watch TV at home. The bathroom had become my personal clinic, with surgical pads on the floor to catch blood and water, a squirt bottle for rinsing, a cup stocked with medicated wipes, a variety of towels, and a pile of bulky sanitary pads. I felt so tired that I didn't know how new mothers possibly had the strength to care for their babies. It took energy to go back and forth to the hospital, sit in the nursery, and pump milk, but at least I could sleep at night and didn't have to pick up a baby. No wonder people had their mothers come and stay with them. The bleeding tired me, bleeding and cleaning up blood. The episiotomy made walking difficult—turning over in bed still hurt. Why did people suggest buying a pretty nightgown for a new mother? She'd just bleed all over it. I felt relieved when I'd finished attending to my body and could put on old pajamas.

Fred had picked up his mother and taken her out to dinner. He was tired, but going out to dinner after a day at the hospital was a Leebron family tradition. When Norman, Fred's father, had been in the hospital in Milwaukee after bypass surgery with complications, the family had gone out to dinner every night. He'd stayed in St. Mary's Hospital for three months, and the family occupied several rooms in an apartment hotel. Fred and I flew home from Portugal, where we were living that summer, and stayed for a month. After the initial bypasses, Norm had infections, and seven additional surgeries. Even on calmer days there was often an unpleasant event, like a tracheostomy, once performed by a resident who became flustered and stopped midway through the procedure. Yet after a day at the hospital, the family always went out. They must have eaten at nearly every restaurant in Milwaukee—one night we drove half an hour to a Hungarian place. Their ability to keep up spirits, to sit and talk together at the end of every day, impressed me. That Carol and Fred had gone out to dinner after the hospital made me happy, even as he grumpily got into bed that night.

"How was dinner?"

"Fine."

"What did you have?"

"Some crab thing. I wasn't exactly hungry."

"Is she getting on your nerves?"

"She's my mother, of course she's getting on my nerves." He turned on the television. "Did you call yet?"

"No. What did your mom think about the labor and delivery situation?"

"She thinks we ought to sue."

We watched the news in silence. A lawsuit would be a trauma on top of the trauma. Fred called the nursery. Cade was the same. He called George and Denise, as we did every night, to give the day's story. We still hadn't seen them, but talking to them was comforting. Dan Itzkowitz had called them three times, Schwartz had called, and August.

"This Itzkowitz guy is taking it hard," George said.

"He's got no sense of humor," Fred said. "What's new with you guys? When does Stanford start?" He drank a bourbon on ice and settled in to listen, while I watched the end of the news without absorbing any information.

On Tuesday morning the nurse said, "She could wake up any minute." They had discontinued the paralyzing drug pavulon. We all looked at Cade, who could potentially open her eyes or move an arm, not because she needed more pavulon or was in pain, but because she was finished sleeping. "She'll finish her antibiotics today, too. On the down side, she's got a catheter in for urine, and we're concerned about her electrolytes. Also, we expect to transfuse more blood today."

"We've heard worse," Fred said. We smiled at each other across her bed. Our baby might wake up.

The nurse turned to me. "Have you held the baby yet?"

"Held her?" I shook my head. She summoned two nurses from the middle room. They had me sit in a low armchair, pulled up close to the head of the warming bed, and put a pillow on my lap. "You don't think it will disturb her?" I asked.

"She'll be fine." They moved some wires, and a monitor beeped. "We detached the sensor, that's all." The pale blue lines on the screen went flat. The nurses slid a white flannel blanket under the baby and wrapped it around her. They wheeled the IV cart close to me. I held out my arms, stiffly, and the nurse lowered the baby into them. Her head was near my left shoulder. The nurses quickly adjusted her breathing tube so that it curved easily over my left arm. They wheeled the respirator a foot closer. They checked the IV wires to make sure none were tugging. They reattached a sensor for the sat rate monitor.

"Relax your shoulders," one of the nurses said. I let them down and breathed.

Another nurse asked, "Do you have a camera?"

"It broke," I said, trying not to move and disturb the baby, my face frozen in the tilted down position.

"We'll take one." She got the insta-camera from the wall cabinet and hunched down with it. There was a click and flash, and a glossy paper square slid out. Cade didn't move, a tiny limp weight in my arms.

"Her sat rate is low," I said. "Look, Fred."

"It'll go back up," the nurse said soothingly. "It's good for her to be held." The side of her head rested on my left arm. She faced me with her eyes closed. I couldn't believe she was asleep, and might wake up. Gauze and tape plastered the top of her forehead, holding in place an IV needle with a yellow plastic cap; my mother had hated that one the most, her unicorn needle. To the right of it, a tiny blue tube was taped in place along her head, from her forehead back to where a cowlick curled at the crown, and there it disappeared under tape into her skin. Halfway back, a syringe hung down from the tube like a dangly earring. Her forehead was tinged red as if she were angry, and the rest of her face had a sallow cast. At her mouth, a dozen pieces of clear tape held in place a white plastic fixture, a hard cylinder which the two respirator tubes fed into, and from which one tube entered her mouth. I'd never seen them move the tube, though they removed it every day to suction her airway, bringing up meconium, blood, and now mucous. It was painful for her to have the tube removed and replaced. Part of her chest was bare and her left hand, free of needles for now, rested on it outside the blanket, the fingers slightly curled in. My baby. She was seven days old.

"Her sat rate's high now," Fred said.

"Good." I looked up without moving my head. Maybe she knew me, maybe I comforted her. She could feel my heart beating, my pulse.

"Shall we put her back now?" the nurse asked.

"Okay, little baby," I whispered, not wanting to give her up. Past the tubes and tape, she was mine. "You have to go back to bed now. Mommy loves you." The nurse bent to take her.

In the anteroom, I peeled off the paper gown, my hands trembling. "I'm sweaty," I said.

"Are you okay?"

"Hot in there."

Fred took the gown from me and dropped it in the trash. He put his arm around me as we walked down the hall. "Should I get the car?"

"I want to walk with you."

At home, Fred's mother sorted through papers spread out on the big table. Carol rarely went anywhere without what she called her book, a datebook in a burgundy leather zipper case that was crammed with lists, receipts, informational articles, and various papers. I sat with her at the table. She had the telephone next to her, and the telephone book next to that. "I held the baby," I told her.

"That's great," she said. "What's her oxygen level now?"

"Still 52, but they're talking about lowering it this afternoon."

"Did they say anything about taking her off the respirator?"

"No."

"Did you ask them?"

"No, but maybe I will later."

"What's her blood pressure?"

"Fred," I called down the hall. "What's her blood pressure?"

"110 over 60."

"Is that normal for a baby?" She shook her head. "Sounds low to me."

"I think it's low. Her heart rate is low, too, but they don't seem concerned."

"They're not concerned?"

"I guess it's not her biggest problem."

"Sure, but still."

"I know. Can I get you something to eat, or coffee, juice?"

She waved her hand dismissively. "I had breakfast at the hotel, thanks."

"I'd better go use the breastpump." I called for Fred to come help me hook it up. The nursery door opened and he emerged, chewing on a pen. What had he been doing in there, hiding? I liked Carol's matter-of-factness, but her questions made me feel inadequate, seeming to imply that I should be more aggressive with the nurses and doctors. Fred and I bent over a table, attaching tubing to the funnel and cup.

"What were you doing," I whispered.

"Nothing," he said quietly, with a defensive twitch of his left shoulder. "Is that okay?"

"Fine. Can you get sandwiches for lunch?"

"Fine. Are you ready?" He handed me the twin funnels.

"Be nice to your mother," I said.

He glared at me. "You be nice to *your* mother."

I held the funnels over my breasts and looked out the window. "Could you put the shade down, please. Everyone can see me."

"We're on the fourth floor, Kathryn. No one can see in."

"They can."

"Cannot." He lowered the shade with a snap. "There. I'll be back in ten minutes."

As he turned to leave, I whispered urgently, "I love you."

"I love you, too," he whispered back angrily. "Now try to relax, or the milk won't come."

"It always comes."

"It won't be as much."

I tried to breathe slowly, and gazed at the photo of Cade on top of the television. That's what one of the nurses had suggested—look at a picture of your baby while you pump. In the next room I could hear Fred and Carol getting ready to go. Their steps sounded down the hall, and the front door opened and shut. Quiet. I'd forgotten to turn on the television. I was hungry, as usual. And tense, as usual. It shouldn't be difficult to arrange to be at the hospital for the two grandparents' visiting hours, and yet it was. Everybody had to be fed, talked to, given keys, directions, explanations. Wasn't it good to have family with us at this time? It must be helping us in ways we didn't realize. I knew I felt proud when I told the nurse, "We've had four out of five grandparents here, all from the East Coast."

At the hospital, we took turns sitting with Cade. When Carol shifted on her stool, I felt anxious that she might be bored. On the telephone, when we were discussing whether she should come, she had said, "It's not like the babies *do* anything," and I had pictured her staring balefully into my nephew Jonathan's isolette for hours on end. She wasn't a sitter—she had too much energy for that, just like my mother. I didn't think either of them could sit still for more than twenty minutes. If Carol ever had the inclination to sit still, she was trained out of it after raising five children. Now she worked as the business manager of a radio station, which meant weekends, and 18-hour days, and she took care of Norm and their big house, and they went to parties and weddings, and traveled, and she always had ten projects going at once—sorting through her mother's belongings, comparison-shopping for a new computer, and researching airfares and villa rentals for a possible family reunion in the Caribbean. She made me feel like an old woman. We discussed all of the monitor readings. She understood the equipment, having been through Milwaukee, and Jonathan, so we could sit and talk easily the way Fred and I did. The baby looked better than stable—she had maintained her saturation rate as the oxygen was lowered.

At the end of the hour, when Carol went to a parents' room to wait for us, Fred and I sat across from each other and a new respiratory therapist came in. He checked the ventilator settings, adjusted a dial, and said, "We're thinking of taking her off the respirator soon."

We both looked up at him. "Taking her off?" I said.

"Yeah, she's doing well, and if we can get the oxygen percentage down to . . ." But I couldn't pay attention because I was trying not to cry, with my chin pinned to my chest, and I was crying anyway.

"Honey?" Fred said.

"I only cry at good news," I managed, noticing that the nurse was observing me surreptitiously. No one cried, or yelled, in the ICN. Everyone spoke calmly and politely and smiled. I recovered myself.

"Now you know," the therapist said, "that if we take her off she might have to go right back on if she doesn't do well."

"Of course," Fred said.

"We'll try by tomorrow, or possibly today. We'll put an oxygen hood on her, she's still not ready for room air. Okay?"

"Okay," one of us said. We had to leave for change of shift. I sniffled, and touched her arm. "Honey, you're doing so well. They're going to try taking you off that machine, so you rest now."

"We'll see you soon, sweetie," Fred said.

In the parents' room, Fred told his mom. "That's amazing," she said, gathering up her papers.

"They say when these cases turn around, they get better fast," I said.

"Though it might not work out," Fred said. "She might have to go right back on the respirator."

She zipped up her case. "That's what happened to Jonathan. They took him off, and then they put him back on."

At home, Carol decided that she would put the crib together. The large wooden slatted pieces leaned against a wall with the mattress and metal springs, and an intimidating assortment of wheels and small metal parts lay on the floor. We had no idea how to assemble the thing. Carol examined all of the pieces, and concluded that she and Fred would go to a baby store and look at cribs on their way to buy groceries. They were back in half an hour, and she laid the large pieces out on the nursery floor and set to work. From the bedroom, where I used the breastpump and then rested on the bed, I could hear bangs and creaks, and after an hour, a light thunk—the mattress being dropped in. I heard her call my sister-in-law Betsy and say, "You're finally home. I just put the crib up—you know you didn't send directions." Betsy had boxed up and sent everything we needed for the baby. We had soft-sculpture animals for the nursery wall, crib sheets, bumpers, and blankets, bottles, toys, bibs, books, and a complete wardrobe of clothes, which waited in two enormous boxes by the nursery window. I went into the nursery. The crib was up. We must have believed by then that Cade would be coming home.

We returned to the hospital in the late afternoon. As we entered the anteroom, we could see her through the window. The bed looked different—there was a clear plastic box, a hood, mounted over the top third of it, over her head. "She's off," Fred said. We stared through the window. There were no tubes coming out of her mouth. There was no ventilator next to the bed. The nurse waved at us.

"We finally get to see you in person, Leeanne," I said.

"Yes." She laughed. She had clipped-short red hair, a plain face.

"It's been great talking with you on the phone," Fred said. "You've been so straightforward with us."

"I'm just glad little Cade is doing well," she said.

I looked at Cade through the hood. Her face! What a sweet mouth, like a little bow. The skin around it was red and irritated. I pointed. "Did the tape do that?"

Leeanne nodded. "It should clear up soon. Did anyone explain to you about the oxygen hood?" Fred and I looked at each other blankly. We were still standing up, too startled by the ventilator being gone to pull over stools and sit. I felt like a student who's forgotten everything instantly.

"Some," Fred said.

"She's having pure oxygen blown on her through that tube." She pointed to a thick, ribbed brown tube that fit through a hole at the top of the hood. "Now she *is* off the pavulon, so you might see her move. She's sleepy because of the morphine—her throat will be sore for a few days from the tube, so she's still on morphine, a smaller dose. Also, she'll be receiving a blood transfusion this afternoon, which will take three hours. Do you have any questions?"

We shook our heads. Fred motioned for me to sit on the side Cade faced.

"She opened her eyes earlier," Leeanne said. "Maybe she'll open them again."

"When she wakes up," I said. "I bet she'll be mad."

"Oh yes." Leeanne smiled. "She might be angry." We all smiled at the thought of Cade waking up and yelling. I'd never heard her make a sound.

"All those days of not crying," Fred said. "Honey, you can be mad at us all you want."

"Us is right." I laughed.

"You're the ones who will get to hear it," Leeanne said.

I noticed an open folder next to her, on an empty warming bed. "Is that," I pointed, "an article on meconium aspiration?" Leeanne looked over at it and hesitated. "I know they're not written for parents. That looks like one we've read. Could we?"

She picked up the folder. "They certainly aren't written for parents."

"No. They're not exactly reassuring, but we like that."

"Well," she said uneasily. "Of course you can read them." She handed me the folder. Why did she hesitate? For a week, we'd been questioning doctors, nurses, and respiratory therapists. In order to learn anything about the causes and outcomes of our baby's condition, we'd had to depend on the director of medical affairs at my mother's company, and on the articles Shane and Jane had copied for us. That article in a folder, just out of reach, made manifest what we'd felt: they had information, but didn't want to give it to us.

Part of a nurse's job in the ICN, as I felt, is to assess the parents' state of mind. Nurses must assess the maturity level of the parents, the degree of parental self-esteem, the support system available to them in the way of family, friends, and religion. They must determine the parents' experience with well and ill infants, and the parents' knowledge of their infant's condition and treatment. I wasn't aware of these nursing responsibilities. I just felt watched. Were we polite enough? Too polite? Friendly? Relaxed? Knowledgeable? Were we coping properly? Were we smart? What were our parents like? What was our background? Who were we? Did we believe in God? What should we be told? I took an article and passed the folder to Fred.

"We have this one," Fred said.

"Oh, I've read that," I said. Leeanne seemed to relax. None of the information was especially new, with publication dates from 1979 to 1989. This was what Cade's medical team was reading? I'd read this stuff, and it left a lot unanswered, such as which respirator settings worked to keep the baby breathing. No wonder Dr. Hanover stood over her day and night. There was only one article we hadn't read, and it wasn't newer or more informative, except for one statistic. It included the mortality rate for severe meconium aspiration syndrome: 78 percent.

"Did you see this?" I said lightly to Fred, holding out the article with my finger on the number, out of the nurse's sight.

"Yes," he said. "Yes I did."

"So," I said. "She's doing pretty well."

"Yes," he said. "Very well."

I handed the folder back to Leeanne. "Thanks a lot. We'd read most of them, but there was one new one."

"Good," she said, but I could tell she would rather not have let us read them. She'd made a mistake leaving the folder open. It actually was a nurse's responsibility to inform parents about their baby's illness, but not by giving them grim articles from medical journals.

Leeanne, Fred and I sat in silence, watching Cade breathe. Her chest rose and fell to her own rhythm now, not a machine's. Maybe Cade would drink milk, I thought, since she didn't have a tube in her mouth anymore. "Will she get milk?"

"She probably will," Leeanne said, considering. "You have milk in the freezer?"

Fred nodded. "A lot."

"We were told it would be given to her in the order I expressed it," I said. "I don't know if she'll start on colostrum, or—"

"Probably so." She looked over my shoulder. "Here's Dr. Meegan."

"Hiya." Dr. Meegan smiled grandly at us. "So we took her off that respirator, and she's doing great, huh?"

"They were wondering about giving the baby breastmilk," Leeanne said.

He nodded approvingly at me. "Why don't we start tomorrow. Let her rest a bit tonight. Have you seen her eyes open?" We shook our heads. "Oh, she was looking all around earlier. It was great to see. How you folks doing?"

"Great." I smiled.

"She's looking good." He gave us a thumbs-up as he passed into the next room. *She looked at* me *first*, I thought, and then, *How does his wife stand him?*

Leeanne told us that Cade would be fed through a tube down her throat, called gavage, since she wouldn't be strong enough to nurse. The babies didn't like it, but it was the best way—milk went right into their stomachs. I looked at Cade. There was one unpleasant procedure after another for her. An eyelid fluttered. I saw a bit of white.

"Did you see that?" I said to Fred.

"What?"

"Her eye, it fluttered."

He got off his stool and came around to my side. We both stared intensely at her. "Will you open your eyes, honey?"

"You don't have to," I said.

"If you want to open your eyes, you can," Fred said. Her head moved, a slight jerk to the side. I could see her whole face, her whole beautiful nose and mouth without tubes or tape, all of her cheeks, her chin.

"Do you think she has a big nose?" I said.

"No." Fred sat back down on his stool. "I don't."

"Our baby is sleeping." I felt thrilled that she wasn't paralyzed but asleep. Then she opened her eyes, slowly, both of them. "They're open," I said, and Fred jumped up and came around. She looked exactly as she had when she was put on my chest at birth, wise and inexpressibly silly. Those days when her eyes were closed, I'd held that image.

"I'm your mom," I whispered.

"I'm your dad." We bent close, separated from her only by the clear plastic of the oxygen hood. "We love you honey," he said.

"You've been so brave." She closed her eyes. "Sit here," I told Fred, indicating my stool. "I'll get your mom." It was seven o'clock in the evening, grandparents' visiting hour. I found Carol in the parents' room.

"She opened her eyes," I said. "Maybe she'll open them for you."

"Don't you want to stay in there?"

"I'll come in later. I'm going to call my parents." I left her and hurried in small steps down the hall. It felt good to let out some energy. It was almost unbearable to sit in the nursery on a stool, with tension in my chest, with wanting to laugh, or shout. I called my mother and sister, then my father. We still had no timetable, no prognosis, I told them. Her hematocrit was low, so she was getting a second blood transfusion at the moment. But they might give her milk tomorrow. And she opened her eyes, and she had Cecily's mouth exactly. I was happy my parents had seen her, that my mom had brought one of the Polaroids home for Cecily, so they all felt how amazing it was that the baby could wake up and drink milk. She wouldn't rest in a perpetual false sleep, her spirit invisible, only her features available for study, as if she were sculpture. Our baby, who had kicked so continually inside me, could move. One night when I was six months pregnant there was a small earthquake at three a.m. and as we stood in the doorway for safety my adrenaline raced; the baby had kicked me steadily for two hours after that. She had kicked, she was a body, but she was "the baby" then, a relative "it" to me then. Now she was a particular "she," a person, and she would respond, she would move. She would be whole.

We drove Carol back to the hotel later and stood on the side-walk together. She wore jeans and a sweater and lace-up walking shoes, and carried everything she needed, a windbreaker and a shoulder bag bulging with papers; but at that moment she appeared frail and tired. Her preparedness seemed an elaborate defense. It was a long trip out here, and the visit wasn't restful. Norman wasn't with her. They loved to travel together. He didn't walk well, he had to take pills and she had to remind him, he always wanted to eat more than he should and she scolded him and slapped bread out of his hands at restaurants. But he protected her, engaged her. He yelled at rude waiters, and when they went to Portugal he would happily drive six hours to a pottery warehouse if she wanted to buy plates. Alone, Carol seemed less sure of herself and less happy. We probably didn't seem very welcoming. I had never found a way to let her know how much I liked spending time with her. She was brisk, brusque, tough, defensive—and extremely sensitive. She called me Miss Kathryn. She must have thought I was prissy and cold. I hugged her goodbye. Fred accompanied her into the bed-and-breakfast, a dark Victorian rowhouse. He got into the car with a sigh.

"What time will you pick her up in the morning?"

"6:45."

"We're almost done. We'll be alone again."

"I know." He drove in silence.

"Oh—I said this thing to the nurse and wondered if your mom mentioned it. The nurse said, 'So all the grandparents came, huh?' and I said, 'Yup, everyone's come out,' and your mother just stared at me and said, 'Norman couldn't come,' and I felt awful. I didn't mean to forget him."

"Nope, she didn't say a word."

"I'm sure she'll tell Betsy."

"Don't worry about it."

"I hate that, I hate saying the wrong thing."

"Kathryn, please. Relax."

"Fine." I crossed my arms. "The thermos handle broke today."

"It did?"

"Snapped right off and I can't get it back on. Might need glue."

"I'll have a look at it," he said, like a regular suburban husband. We'd won the thermos in a dance contest at the Holiday Inn in Laredo, Texas. We'd traveled overland from Guatemala and were entering the United States to resume our ordinary life of part-time work to support the writing. We'd visit friends in Austin, then fly to Portland, where we thought we might live. We could get teaching jobs and buy a house there someday, have a dog, and children. We didn't end up living there. We surveyed the aluminum-sided houses set back from wide leafy streets, and decided that we'd rent one of those houses and mow the lawn and set up the barbecue and drink ourselves to death: we weren't ready for suburban life. Sometimes I knew acutely how much our life oppressed Fred. Since I'd been pregnant he'd worked more and more hours, for three nonprofit organizations and for Cal State Hayward, where he taught two fiction workshops. He was writing a novel on the commuter train. I teased him that he needed a rich, expatriate wife who didn't want children.

In Laredo, the local travel agents had thrown a pool party for themselves, but hardly anyone showed up, so they invited the hotel guests. Fred won a free breakfast for us by naming the year the Titanic sank. For the dance contest, the deejay played "Shout," three times. We put our hands up when the song commanded us, danced low and meditatively in the quiet stretches, and sang the backup parts. We didn't win the all-expense-paid trip for two to Houston; they gave that to a travel agent. We won the handsome green-and-white Coleman picnic thermos, which we carried to San Francisco, as proof that we could still work hard and be rewarded. We'd been welcomed home. Who knew that one year later it would be the perfect container for transporting breastmilk?

7

The next morning, we happened to ride the elevator with my regular obstetrician. She appeared startled at the sight of us. "How's your baby doing?" she asked.

"Better now," I said, taken aback. I hadn't spoken with her since my last office visit.

"It was a surprise," she said. "They weren't expecting meconium."

"No," Fred said. "Apparently not."

When we got off the elevator, we murmured to each other: surprise, huh, no kidding, big surprise. My obstetrician with her perfect blunt-cut blond hair, her impeccable lab coat. I used to feel disheveled when I went to see her, having taken two buses to get there. She stood very straight and said little. She wore neutral lipstick and discreet gold earrings. Her round blue eyes rarely blinked as she looked me over. I'd bring a list of questions to ask, because she worked quickly and would be out the door within five minutes of her entrance if I didn't arrest her with a question. She was competent, though, and where was she when the baby came? What was the point of soliciting recommendations and choosing a doctor, when whoever happened to be on duty delivered the baby? The way she'd vanished behind the closing elevator door and left us to our messy life felt typical.

A new nurse sat at the head of Cade's bed, a middle-aged Asian woman. We'd heard her talking in the middle nursery room a few nights before, boring a younger nurse with a lecture on why she believed in reincarnation. "Hi Mom, Hi Dad," she said.

"Hi," Fred said. "How's the baby?"

"Just waking up. Mom can change her diaper now."

We stood in the baby's field of vision as her eyes opened. "Hi sweetie, it's Mom and Dad," Fred said. We bent over her and touched her arm. Did she know us?

"You go ahead then," the nurse said. I unfastened the side tapes and opened the diaper, which was wet. I slid it out from under her and threw it in the trashcan by the sink. The nurse directed me to the shelf under her bed, where I found disposable thin cotton towels. She had me wet one at the sink. Then I wiped the baby, front to back, and reached down for a new diaper.

"Mom has got a lot to learn." The nurse took the fresh diaper from under my hand. "You've got to clean her much better than that. Let me show you." My face was hot as I stepped back. She wet another cotton towel and held it up. "The whole diaper area must be cleaned." She handed me the towel. I stepped up to the bed. She stood behind me and to the side, watching around me. I wiped a broader area than I had before, the whole buttocks and the tops of the baby's thighs. "You need practice," she said.

"I'm sure I'll get some." I tried to sound cheerful.

She handed me the diaper. "Do you know how to put this on?"

"Why don't you show me?" I stepped aside and handed the diaper back to her. She shook it open with a crackle and briskly slid it under Cade, pulled up the front, and fastened the tapes tightly.

"Nice and snug," she said. "Next time you put it on."

"Yes, ma'am."

Fred and I sat next to each other so we could both see Cade's face. "You have such beautiful eyes," I said to her.

"You'll try breastfeeding later today," the nurse said. "If they okay it at rounds." She lifted her clipboard and made a few notes. "Nina wants to see you this morning."

Fred was examining the wires and monitors. "Have they discontinued the dopamine?"

"Earlier." She hummed to herself as she wrote on the clipboard.

"She's just on the glucose."

"That's right."

"Does she get electrolytes, too?" he said. "Dr. Hanover mentioned an electrolyte imbalance."

"She gets them as necessary." She lifted her face and looked Fred in the eye, then went back to work. She wouldn't be saying anything else.

We sat in silence for a while, until the baby closed her eyes, and then we left the nursery. As we crossed the hall to Nina's office I whispered, "*You* change the diaper next time."

The social worker ushered us into low chairs. "How are you two doing?"

"Fine," I said. "We're more rested."

"Good. A *lot* of changes for you." She shook her head. "Cade is much improved, yes? You must be happy to see her off the respirator."

Fred nodded. "Very."

"They are thinking about discharge early next week or even this weekend if she continues to do well." Fred and I looked at each other. No one had mentioned the possibility of discharge to us. "I thought you might want to spend the night tonight, and maybe tomorrow, since you are to begin breastfeeding, no? Is it today?" She turned over several pages. "Today, right?"

"If they okay it at rounds," I said, feeling as if my breasts had become another medication or piece of equipment.

"Let's plan on tonight then." She wrote a note to herself. "And second, I wanted to give you the brochure for the Golden Gate program." Fred and I read it together: *Golden Gate Regional Center Prevention Program: Do you have questions about your baby's development?*

"We refer all of our high-risk babies to Golden Gate," Nina explained. "The program follows children up to age three and tracks their development. It's federally funded, it's free to you, and it's your choice whether to enroll."

"Tracks their development as far as—" I searched for the right word. These ideas—breastfeeding, discharge, a high-risk babies program—were being presented as if we'd discussed all of the issues beforehand. But we hadn't, had we? "As far as brain damage?"

"Cade has done so well," she said emphatically. "It's for your own reassurance. The eye and hearing exams will be six weeks after discharge, we'll take care of scheduling those, let me just make a note." She wrote on a pad.

Fred leaned forward. "The eye and hearing exams are for?"

"The respirator babies. There's not much chance of damage with a full-term baby, but we like to check it out."

"It's the pure oxygen," I said. "That could injure them?"

"Right." She nodded comfortably. "But the doctors are really pleased."

"Are they?" I felt as if we hadn't talked to a doctor in days.

"She's made excellent progress." Nina's Caribbean accent, the lilting elongation of the words, and her low-toned voice seemed designed to induce relaxation.

"We need more sterile water jars," I said.

"Let me get you a twelve-pack." She rose from her chair. "Do you need labels?"

"Yes," Fred said. We watched her walk out the door.

"It's good she can be enrolled," I said.

"It's good," Fred said. "Those jerks."

We went home for rounds and I sat at our work table with *The Merck Manual.* Fred read the newspaper next to me. One of our medical articles had mentioned cerebral palsy as a risk. I'd always thought cerebral palsy was an inherited disease, but the syndromes were defined as nonprogressive motor disorders resulting from central nervous system damage before or during birth, characterized by an impairment of voluntary movement.

"I'll be damned," I said. "Birth trauma, asphyxia, and jaundice are three of the causes. What was Jonathan's problem?"

"Oral cerebral palsy," Fred said. "He had difficulties speaking."

His speech was much improved, but Jonathan did sometimes garble his words. He had a speech therapist. Betsy had done exhaustive research, found a good preschool for him, joined parents' support groups, and collaborated on a video project about children with his problem. His problem. I didn't even know the whole story, and I was a relative.

The work of parenting seemed all-consuming and invisible. We were new parents, which was shocking enough. Other parents would smile at us and we would smile back; people without children wouldn't know anything about our lives. *Let me be sexy again,* I thought. Let me not go to the mall in a sweatsuit. Let me not allow the furniture to become encrusted with baby food—I used to clean houses and I recalled chipping dried baby food off a mahogany table with a butter knife. *Let me be part of the life I've known.*

Now we were being thrust into a more specialized role, as parents of a child with problems. I didn't want to read any more, about maximal independence, associated handicaps, and the burden on families. The baby was going to live, and that had been the whole question her first week: life, or death. Make it or not make it. Turn the corner. She'd turned the corner.

I read about involvement of the arms and legs, slow writhing movements that increase with emotional tension, incoordination, and convulsive seizures. Some children had normal intelligence and some suffered mental retardation. It was difficult to diagnose cerebral palsy in early infancy, and children at risk needed close follow-up observation. These children, the manual said, would reach their maximal potential only with the help of stable and sensible parental care combined with the assistance of public and private agencies.

"This is a long haul," I said to Fred. "You don't even know much until the second year."

"Mmhmm," he said, from behind the sports section.

I shut the book. You could join a support group, but you might be alone with the people you loved. Would my mother understand? Would she not want to hear? I could already imagine myself exaggerating the baby's gloomy prospects so it would seem dramatic, so she would pay attention. *I must be a very superficial person*, I thought, and I was. What does she look like? my mother had asked. Oh she's beautiful, I'd said. She's lovely. And underneath, the ragged little thought trailed: *What if she weren't beautiful? Would you still love her? Would you have to learn to love her?*

As we walked into the ICN after rounds, the nurse said, "Ready to breastfeed, Mom?"

"Sure," I said. Calling the parents Mom and Dad must have saved her the trouble of learning names.

"She tolerated milk, so Dr. Meegan gave the go-ahead."

"Did you do gavage?" I said.

"That's right, Mom. You know about that."

"We do," Fred said. She made a mark on her clipboard.

The baby would breathe room air for short periods, and they thought she could handle it. For the first time, I didn't wear a yellow paper gown in the nursery but a cotton hospital gown that opened at the front. I sat in a low armchair. Cade was sleeping. The nurse stopped the glucose IV solution temporarily; the needle stayed in the baby's hand, attached to a short length of capped-off tubing. She disconnected the heart and blood pressure monitors, wrapped the baby in a white flannel blanket, and handed her to me. I held her so she was lying on one side, facing me, and I pulled open the gown to expose a breast.

"Comfortable?" the nurse asked. I was struggling to hold the baby horizontal. "Let me get you a pillow." She placed a large bed pillow underneath the baby to fill the space between her and my lap.

"That's better," I said. "But she's asleep."

"Let's stimulate her rooting reflex." She rubbed her index finger along the baby's cheek. I tried it, too. The baby didn't wake. She pried open the closed mouth. She put her hand at the back of the baby's head and pushed her mouth onto my nipple. The baby's mouth stayed limply open, but she didn't suck. The nurse looked displeased. "She sucks on a pacifier. Okay—let's give her to Dad."

"What do I do?" Fred said. The nurse took the baby from me. I closed my gown and got up. Fred sat down and I put the pillow in his lap. He held out his arms, the way I had, as if to receive a load of logs for the fireplace. The nurse laid the baby across his arms. It seemed he hardly breathed. I stood over him.

"Bring her in," I said, the expert now, and he slowly relaxed his arms and brought her close.

He cradled her and said, "I'm your Dad."

A nearby nurse said, "Oh, how sweet."

Would we never have a private moment with our baby?

Later we tried again. "She's awfully sleepy," I said. I stuck my finger in Cade's mouth and it opened but then shut. I opened it and put it right over my nipple. Nothing. Another nurse was called over from the middle room.

"Frances nursed all of her five kids."

"Five?" I repeated as Frances came close. She looked much sturdier and healthier than I could ever hope to be.

"Time to get down and dirty," Frances said. "When they won't get on at first, you have to trick them. Express a little milk so it's on the nipple." I did that. A third nurse came over to watch; she leaned against an empty warming bed. "And let's try a different hold, the football." She had me tuck the baby to my right side, facing up, with my arm under her. "That might wake her up," she said. "Express more milk." I pressed with my thumb and finger on the areola and milk bloomed out on the nipple.

"She's got the milk," the third nurse said.

Frances opened Cade's mouth and put it over the nipple. "Put your other hand here," she directed, pressing my left hand at the back of her head to keep her close. She stroked the baby under the chin, quick short strokes back toward the throat. "Makes them want to swallow." The baby gave a suck and then went slack.

"She did it!" I said. But the nurses looked dissatisfied, with their arms crossed.

"Let's try the other side," Frances said. We repeated all of the maneuvers on the left side. The baby sucked for a few seconds and then stopped. Frances looked down at her. "She's got to latch on."

The baby was panting. Fred said, "Maybe we should let her rest now."

"Nothing else we can do," the nurse said.

"How are her fluids today?" Fred asked.

"Better. But she's losing weight."

In the parents' room, we whispered. "I feel self-conscious in there," I said.

"And why is that?" Fred said. "Just because all the nurses are standing around and staring at you?"

I wouldn't smile. "It's hard to relax. I should be relaxed. And they're not very patient. All the books say that even normal babies can have trouble getting started, and that mothers shouldn't feel discouraged."

"I know."

"What do they expect? They're acting like it's such a big problem that she can't do it."

"It's not as if she's used to room air or anything."

"True," I said. "Help me hook this up. My breasts are killing me." Fred attached the tubing to the machine and funnel and screwed on the cup. "We forgot the sterile water jars," I said, suddenly upset.

"Honey, you've got to relax. I'll get one from the nurse." He went into the hall.

I called after him, "She won't be happy with you!"

He came back in with a jar of water and emptied it into the bathroom sink. "I don't care if the nurse is happy or not," he said. "This is about us and our baby. You're not getting enough rest. I think we should go home and you should take a nap."

"We have to go home to pack for tonight anyway," I said.

Fred pointed at himself. "I will pack," he said, and pointed at me. "You will sleep." That made me feel less tense. If we both took a nap, I couldn't sleep because I felt there were things that needed to get done. If Fred took a nap and I worked, I felt satisfied to accomplish a household task—straightening the living room or doing the dishes—but I resented him for sleeping. Why couldn't we sleep at the same time and take comfort in each other? Why couldn't I allow us to give in to our tiredness for an hour in the afternoons?

We went home to unpack and repack the hospital bag. "Here are those sugarless lollipops," I said. "Gee, they really came in handy." Fred laughed; I'd checked every store in the neighborhood for lollipops that wouldn't make me thirsty during labor.

"This is the only thing I feel bad about," he said, picking out the unused washcloth. "I was supposed to wipe your face with a cool cloth." He folded it into his hand.

"Honey," I said. "I don't think it would have made a difference."

We pulled up stools and sat by the bed. The new nurse had given the baby formula through a feeding tube, not realizing we had breastmilk in the freezer. Cade slept, her head turned toward me, her mouth fallen open. She had cried herself to sleep, after having been stuck repeatedly by the nurse, who tried and failed to start a new IV in the baby's right foot; after forty minutes, she had called in another nurse to assist. The tiny veins were difficult to find, especially since Cade's hands and feet were swollen.

Neither of us spoke for a while. All of the work with the breastpump, the sterilizing, the pumping, the labeling, the depositing in the nursery freezer—and she gave our baby formula. The idea that she'd be given the milk in the order in which I'd pumped it, starting with colostrum, had been reassuring, as if normalcy could be restored to her.

Finally Fred said, "How are her blood gases?"

"They're okay. She's doing well."

"What time do you think we should try breastfeeding?" I asked.

"Around ten o'clock would be good."

I left the nursery and entered the other anteroom, where the freezer was. I thought about discarding my gown and then rescrubbing and gowning when I went back in, but that seemed excessive. I felt tired of being scrupulous about rules. I squatted down in front of the small freezer. There must have been fifty bottles of my milk in there. The unit assistant, an older Nordic-looking woman with a high blond ponytail, turned to me.

"I put all of yours on the middle shelf."

"Thanks. I thought I'd arrange them in order, since she's getting milk now."

"Don't worry, we'll do that."

"Okay, thanks." I stayed there a moment, studying the bottles, all of our handwritten labels. 8:10 a.m., 2:56 p.m. How quaint, to be so specific. The nurses probably thought we were ridiculous. Why not 8 a.m., 3 p.m., or even morning, and afternoon? The milk looked weird frozen, separated into thick opaque layers, some appearing bluish, others yellow. Milk from other mothers crowded the top and bottom shelves, but no one had nearly as much milk as we did. Why not? Surely some of the preemies were here for weeks, or even months. Maybe their babies could drink it sooner and a huge backlog didn't develop. It felt too intimate to be examining other mothers' milk. I shut the freezer door.

We sat with Cade until nine. Sometimes she opened her eyes, and she even opened her hands, and we put our fingers against her palm, and she tightened her fingers.

"She's holding my finger," one of us would say, astonished. Her eyes were dark blue, and round, and she seemed to look right at me, into me, as she had when she was born, as if she could see beyond the skin of my cheek, behind the bone, into a black essential space that was me.

Jim Spicer, the respiratory therapist, came in. "You're back," I said. "I thought you'd left for Thailand."

"Not yet. Just a few days off." He checked the ventilator settings for the oxygen hood, then nodded toward the baby. "Can you believe this?"

Fred shook his head. "It's incredible."

"We really didn't know," Jim said, and his eyes darted to the left for a second. "She was sick."

"She's done amazingly well," I said. "Thanks to all of you."

"Well." He shrugged awkwardly. "She sure pulled through. Once she turned that corner, she kept right on going."

"We're having trouble with the breastfeeding," I said.

He looked at his shoes, then up at the nursery wall behind me. "She'll have a sore throat from the ventilator tube for, oh, at least a few days. That won't help. And then she's tired, too. She still needs that oxygen hood."

We set ourselves up in the parents' room, finding sheets and blankets on the linen shelves down the hall. Since our bad backs wouldn't tolerate the sofabed, we made a bed on the floor. I changed into pajamas. The room felt cozy as I sat on the couch and ate a banana, read a fashion magazine. How odd it was to stay at the hospital, and to prepare for bed when the staff was still working. The new shift would start at 11:30. It was a relief to be there, though, away from our telephone, close to our baby, as we should be. A relief to be in this too-small, artificially homelike room, to have our surroundings reflect the strangeness of our life these days. We had normalized our life as much as possible, keeping the house clean, shopping, returning telephone calls. We paid our bills and watched late-night television, and put on fresh clothes in the morning. But to be in this room felt real. Outside our bedroom door was the perpetually operating ICN, like a factory or, as one nurse called it, a hatchery.

At ten o'clock, when we went in to try breastfeeding again, Cade looked different. The light around her bed was different, gray instead of golden; the warming lamps weren't on. The entire warming bed was gone, with its overhead fixtures. Cade lay asleep in a clear plastic bassinet, swaddled in a white flannel blanket.

"The oxygen hood," Fred said.

There was no barrier between us. She lay peacefully in the bassinet, as if it had always been her bed. "She's just breathing air," I said. There was space around her, with no lamps overhead, no ventilator next to the bed. She wore only two wires, for the heart rate and blood pressure monitors, and one IV, for the glucose solution. The nurse unhooked her easily and handed her to me as I sat in the low chair.

Of course she was asleep. This time, though, she awoke and gave a small, raspy cry.

"That's her sore throat," the nurse said, smiling. "She'll get louder."

"Poor baby, can't even cry," I said, stroking her chest. I put her mouth on the nipple and she sucked for a few seconds, stopped, then sucked again. She gave another hoarse cry and fell asleep.

"Do you think she's getting any milk?" Fred said.

The nurse shrugged. "She's still on the glucose, so she won't starve."

We set our alarm clock for one o'clock and four o'clock feedings. I liked the nursery at night. The two anterooms were brightly lit, and at the desks the staff read files and test results. Inside, low lights made the nursery pale blue, with soft punctuations of reading lamps, and monitor screens with glowing numbers in red, blue, and green. A radio played country music at a low volume. Leeanne was tightly tucking a second blanket over Cade when we walked in. "It helps the babies feel secure," she said. "Cade has been irritable tonight." Nurses talked quietly in the middle room. There were no other visitors, no doctors coming through on rounds, no one bathing crying babies. I sat in the low chair and tried to feed her, and again she sucked for a few seconds and stopped.

"She's got a good sucking reflex," Leeanne said. "She's been sucking on her fingers."

"She's hungry."

"Before you came in, she was smacking her lips."

I laughed at that. Each time I tried nursing, she stayed on for a little longer. The nursery was peaceful and private at night. I was tired, but gratified to be doing the normal thing parents did when they had a new baby, getting up at night for feedings.

"I like her t-shirt, Leeanne," I said.

"I picked it out myself," she said with a smile. It was a hospital-issue long-sleeved one.

"What ever became of her umbilical catheter?" Fred asked.

"Dr. Meegan pulled it."

"No more blood gases?" I said. I'd come to depend on them. How would we know if she was breathing well?

"They'll do a heelstick now and then."

After the 7:30 a.m. attempted feeding, we dressed and packed up. We dropped the sheets in a linen hamper down the hall, and folded the blankets. We went upstairs to the snack bar. Change of shift had just ended and the cafeteria was crowded, so we took our breakfast to the family waiting room next door. We didn't know what people were waiting for—surgery patients, or emergency room, or maternity—but they were in a state of full encampment. A couple lay stretched out, entangled, on a sofa. Someone spoonfed a baby. A woman wore slippers with her clothes. People drank coffee and stared dully at a morning news show. They resembled passengers at the end of an overnight flight, trying to rouse themselves in the stale air. I liked being there, surrounded by fellow travelers.

"The thing is," I said between mouthfuls of muffin, "she doesn't seem hungry."

"She's still on the glucose IV," Fred said.

"You mean, she *isn't* hungry."

"Right. Maybe she should come off the IV."

"Let's say something before rounds. Will you say it?"

"I'll say it," he said tiredly.

We went back downstairs, where Fred demonstrated for the nurse that he knew how to take an axillary temperature, from his days as an orderly, and learned how to change Cade's diaper. When he sat down he looked sweaty. I was directed to change Cade's shirt. I pulled one of her arms through a sleeve, thinking that I hadn't babysat in over ten years. I didn't know what I was doing. But if I moved slowly, and didn't hurt her, it would be all right.

"Very good," the nurse said as I pulled down the shirt.

"She's tolerant," I said.

"She's sweet," the nurse said. "I like being assigned to her." I should hope so, I thought. It had never occurred to me that nurses liked or didn't like being assigned to certain babies. Cade had many different nurses, even though every baby was supposed to have a primary nursing team of four or five. Was Cade everybody's last choice? There were monitors to watch, blood to be drawn every two hours, IVs to check. Just keeping her chart current must have been a lot of work. And she might have died. How did that affect nursing assignments? Maybe people would rather not attend to a baby who might die on their shift. Or maybe the August vacation season made work schedules inconsistent. I felt that fewer nurses would have been better for Cade. Each nurse could be more familiar with the baby, and maybe Cade would be more relaxed if the same hands touched her every day.

Baby Ashley had the same nurse nearly every day. The nurse and Ashley's mother chatted about the baby, about Ashley's brother, about the nurse's weekend plans. They had long conversations, they laughed together. Ashley's mother reached into the baby's isolette easily, authoritatively, to change her diaper, rearrange her toys. We were stiff and unsociable by comparison, two brooders who sat on stools and trembled over every task. Maybe *we* were everybody's last choice.

I changed in the parents' room, into a cotton hospital gown. When I entered the nursery, Fred was holding Cade against his shoulder, one arm and hand supporting her back and neck. His head tilted toward the baby, as if to hold her more firmly in place. I sat in the chair and we tried again. At least the baby was awake. She didn't seem comfortable held across my body, so I awkwardly moved her into the football position. Paul Meegan came in.

"Breastfeeding? Good," he said. "How's it going?"

"Could be better," I said, struggling to put the baby's mouth over my nipple. He stood over me, and I felt self-conscious with my breast exposed. He reminded me of certain premeds I knew in college—he may have taken Bedside Manner 101, he said the lines, he tried to be generous to the lower orders of human being, but he just couldn't help being insensitive. He was six feet tall, and he stood two steps from my chair.

"She's not really sucking, huh?" he said.

"We were thinking," Fred said, "that if she were off the IV she might be more hungry."

He nodded vigorously. "Why don't we just discontinue it." He stared down at Cade, who gave soft, hoarse cries. "Sore throat," he said. "Did we talk about that?"

"Jim mentioned it," I said. "So she doesn't need the glucose?"

"I don't see why she would," Meegan said. "Now that she's getting milk."

"Here," the nurse said, and she pushed the baby's head from behind so her mouth went over my nipple. The baby sucked. I looked down at her intently, willing her to stay on.

Fred diverted Meegan's gaze by saying, "The sore throat will go away in a few days?"

"We'll give her low-dose morphine for another day or so." He tucked his clipboard under his arm. "Rounds," he said, smiling, and ducked into the anteroom. The doctors moved into the middle room and assembled in front of an isolette. Meegan stood with his back to the isolette and began to speak. We could barely hear him talking. "So you see," he was saying. "The real key here . . ." A moment later, he made a bow and said to the nurses, "And you ladies have been superb detectives. If you hadn't found the clues, I never could have . . ." We couldn't hear the rest. The nurses weren't smiling back.

The baby was asleep. "I guess we'll go." I put my face close to hers, so our noses almost touched. Our baby looked almost normal, sleeping in a blanket, not attached to anything, with only a single capped-off IV dangling from the top of her head.

We stopped at the bulletin board on our way to the parents' room. At least fifty photographs of babies were tacked up, with thank-you cards and handwritten letters.

"If it's so obvious about the IV," I whispered. "Then why was she still on it."

"Can't explain that," Fred said.

"Is Meegan an ass or what," I said.

"At least he treats everyone the same way."

The babies in the photographs were fat, huge, healthy. Some sat up, some smiled. "Joshua, 8 months, 16 1/2 pounds!" was written on the edge of a photo, "Amy at 12 pounds!" on another. They must have been preemies. I read a letter, written in large round script: "Thank you so much for all you did. We couldn't have made it without you. Robert is now 14 pounds. Can you believe it?" Would we feel happy and gushy like this? We went into the parents' room. I changed into a t-shirt and drank a cup of water. Although I wanted to take a shower and eat, I didn't especially want to go home.

Fred swung our bag over his shoulder. "Let's get out of here. It's been a long as hell morning."

At home, I stood in our nursery and looked at the baby's things, the soft sculptures of a hippo, a giraffe, a lion, and an elephant that we'd hung on the wall. I liked the hippo best, with its too-close-together blue eyes and floppy ears. The changing table was stocked with cottonballs and wipes and, underneath, our first delivery of cloth diapers. I unpacked some of the smallest clothes from the box by the window—tiny stretchy sleepers, cotton t-shirts, and socks. I carried her sleeping basket into our room and put it on the trunk next to the bed. We'd made a mattress out of a beach towel folded and covered with a thin flannel blanket, a mattress hard enough so she wouldn't smother. She'd sleep in our room for a couple of months. The vista of time had opened again for me, to admit months, instead of hours and days.

The ICN corridor had a festive air. Nurses stood in the doorway of the first anteroom, eating cake off of paper plates. Dr. Hanover came down the hall still chewing. "Mmmm," a nurse said to us. "You guys should help yourselves. The Fiorella family just brought a ton of food—salads and sandwiches and cake." She licked a finger. "We have been pigging out."

"Thanks," we both said. I squeezed past them to put the morning's jar of milk in the freezer.

"Oh you know," the unit assistant said to me. "Since your little girl is going home soon, maybe you don't need to bring in any more."

I held the freezer door open. "Why don't I just leave it for now, since we'll be here for a while."

"Sure," she said. "And when you go, you could even take some of the other milk with you. It keeps in your freezer at home for a week."

"Great." I hurried out. Fred was putting our bag under a couch in the parents' room. "They want us to take our milk home," I said.

"It's in their way?"

"You should see how much we have compared to everyone else." I felt close to crying. It had taken a long time to feel comfortable in the ICN, to feel that we belonged, weren't intruding.

Cade was awake when we went into the nursery. She was wrapped in a white blanket but her hands were free. When I put my pinky on her palm, she closed her fingers. She wore a white t-shirt, and a pink-and-blue striped knit cap.

"They discontinued the IV," Fred said.

The nurse looked up from her clipboard. "She's off everything. They're thinking of a Saturday discharge."

"Saturday," I said. In two days. I couldn't quite believe it. I was accustomed to our routine, and had prepared myself to continue living this way indefinitely. We could manage the role of being ICN parents—we were just getting good at it. We examined the baby. She had small, dark blue bruises on the backs of both hands.

"She has bruises on her feet, too, and on her head," the nurse said. "But they'll go away soon."

Aside from the bruises, she appeared unharmed. The premature babies in the nursery were skinny and reddish. Next to them, Cade looked enormous and plump and creamy. The IV cart was gone. The respirator was gone. The oxygen hood was back up on a shelf in the anteroom. Only the heart rate monitor remained, and she wasn't attached to it at the moment. We could move around her bed without worrying about wires or equipment. She could move. She could move her head from side to side, and open and close her hands.

Jim came by to visit. "I sure was glad to see that umbilicus catheter go."

"The umbilicus tube?" I said. "Why's that?"

"Well," he hedged. "You know, risk of infection with an invasive tube."

"Ah." We'd never considered the risks associated with the tube coming out of her bellybutton. What infections could she have gotten? I felt the flicker of panic in my chest of averted danger. There was respiratory crisis, pneumonitis, loss of blood pressure, and hole in the lung—the life-threatening ones. There was lack of oxygen to the brain—the complicating one. Other problems we didn't know about: umbilical catheters carry risks of hemorrhage and central nervous system damage as well as infection.

"When's Thailand?" I said.

"Two weeks." He pretended to swing a golf club. "Can't wait."

Cade gave a small cry. "Let's try the breast," the nurse said. Jim bobbed and waved and went to check his respirator babies. I sat in the chair. Fred picked up Cade easily and placed her in my arms. "Let's try skin-to-skin contact," the nurse said, pulling my gown open so my stomach was bare. Cade gave a short squall, and I put her mouth on my breast. She sucked. "Tummy to tummy. You should try it at home. Having her skin touching yours is important for bonding." I didn't like to think about bonding, since everyone talks about the precious hours after birth, how crucial it is for the family to be together, the wonder of the first breastfeeding, etcetera. Once I'd turned on the TV while pumping milk, to hear T. Berry Brazelton lovingly describing those irreplaceable first minutes between mother and child, in words that sounded only cruel to me.

"Hi Mom, hi Dad," the Asian nurse said after change of shift. She spoke abruptly but cheerfully, almost barking out her words. With that voice, and her short wiry hair, she reminded me of a gym teacher. I thought she'd like to wear a whistle around her neck. She picked up a clipboard. "So you've done changing the diaper, changing the t-shirt, lifting, holding, putting baby on back, putting baby on stomach, and the bath," she said.

"We watched a bath," I said.

Cade opened her round eyes. "Hi sweetie," Fred said.

"Observed bath." The nurse made a mark. "But no taking temperature or swabbing umbilicus, right?"

"I took her temperature." Fred touched Cade's palm with his fingertip. She closed her fingers around it. "You try," he said to me, and I put my finger there but she wouldn't hold on.

"She won't do it for me," I said.

"She only does it once, that's all," Fred said. "Next time you try first."

The nurse said, "Dad, show me how you do it." She handed him the thermometer. He shook it down, then slid the baby's t-shirt off her shoulder and started to put the thermometer under her arm.

"It's better to take her arm out of the sleeve."

"I didn't do that before."

"It's better."

Fred gently pulled the sleeve off Cade's arm and positioned the thermometer. After four minutes he read the temperature, and she made a mark on her clipboard. He put her sleeve back on.

"Mom," she said. "Let's swab the umbilicus. It needs to be cleaned once a day with a sterile wipe or it will get infected." The stub was black and knotty, like the burnt end of a rope. "You have to get in there, all around it, and wipe away the dried blood." She handed me a medicated cloth. As I started wiping, tentatively, dark brown flecks collected on the cloth. "All around," she insisted. I manipulated the stub so I could get under it, pushing it gently from side to side, and finally the skin around the stub was clean and the cloth was full of flecks. "You get an A for that." She marked her clipboard. How many items were on that checklist anyway?

"Now we'll try nursing," she said, and I had a sudden memory of Girl Scout camp. After an hour of swimming, we'd hear a whistle, which meant we were allowed to get out of the cold pool in the middle of the woods. We'd stand shivering in front of the instructor, who wore a warm-up suit and looked perfectly comfortable, and she'd yell, Volleyball in five—hustle!

Cade wasn't hungry. I put her on and she sucked and then fell off right away. When the nurse went to prepare a bottle, I rolled my eyes at Fred.

"You're doing great," he said softly.

"Do I get an A?" I whispered. He shook his head disgustedly and stretched out his arms, uncramping himself from the tense posture he had settled into on the stool.

Dr. Hanover came into the nursery. "Do you think Cade needs an apnea monitor?" I asked.

He wrinkled his nose dismissively. "This baby has done remarkably well. There's no need for a monitor. Just treat her like a normal infant." That stung. Would our anxiety level ever be calibrated correctly?

"I can't believe she's just lying there, breathing air," I said.

Fred asked, "You're not worried about long-term complications?"

He wrinkled his nose again. "She's alert. She has good muscle tone. She'll do fine."

"She'll be in the Golden Gate program," I said.

"Good." He shifted his weight. "So, are you ready to bring her home?"

"Can't wait," Fred said.

"We've been learning all about diapers and feedings and baths," I said.

"It'll be rough." He twinkled his eyes at us. "I remember when mine were babies. You don't sleep." He looked at me. "Have you gotten some rest?"

"I feel good," I said.

"You should enjoy your last night," he said. "Before she comes home. Life will never be the same." He sighed, and strode over to examine Cade's chart. I didn't mind this comment from someone who'd had children, but I'd gotten sick of hearing these things for the past nine months. Appreciate your sleep, people said, because you won't sleep much. Get a lot of writing done now, they said, because you won't write after. Go out now, they said, travel now. Live your life now, because you won't live after. In defense, I'd stored up images of happy parents, parents who traveled, tourist parents with babies in backpacks in Chiang Mai, parents pushing babies in strollers around the plaza in Oaxaca. They looked rested and healthy, and they were having an adventure. Fred's parents took him camping across the country when he was nine months old. My parents took us to England for a year when Cecily was a year old and I was four. I thought of our friends Toma and Kisenija—Kisenija finished her Ph.D. dissertation in the month after Una was born. She said having the baby helped her to concentrate because she had less time, and so she focused her energies on important tasks.

The end of our writing life was predicted most happily from our writer friends without children. Choose children, or choose to write, they said, simple as that. One of my favorite twentieth century poets, Elizabeth Bishop, had no children. Her mentor, Marianne Moore, had none. Anais Nin, Gertrude Stein, Virginia Woolf—none. Sylvia Plath had children, but failed to provide a model for a happy life. It was hard enough to write without drinking and smoking and killing yourself. Subtract your vices, add children, and the equation seemed impossible. I always came back to Kisenija, to how she seemed when we saw her in Iowa City, on our way to California. Over breakfast, two-month-old Una reclined contentedly in a baby swing. Kisenija talked about childbirth, and being a mother, and she made coffee and looked luminous standing by the kitchen window in light filtered through the leaves of a maple tree, almost clarified by her experience. She was utterly relaxed, and she was writing. She laughed and buttered rolls for us. I would be like her, I decided.

8

At five o'clock, the only people in the Star India restaurant were the ones who worked there, men in white dress-shirts and turbans who occupied a table at the back.

"My dad said we should keep a journal," I said, as we sat down. "For legal reasons."

"Betsy said the same thing."

"Do you think we'll sue?"

"I don't know." Fred signaled the waiter. "I'm having a beer."

The waiter appeared and Fred ordered korma and curry and bread, then began writing on a legal pad he kept in his knapsack. I wrote on the tiny notepad I carried. The first page listed phone numbers for when I went into labor—Labor and Delivery, five taxicab companies, three workplace numbers for Fred, numbers for friends in case I couldn't reach him, and the number for Bismarck ambulance service. Then there were items to take to the hospital, and numbers to call for when the baby arrived. The next three pages were filled with notes on meconium aspiration—there were notes on pH levels and alpha-adrenergic blockers. I started this journal with the current day, August 6, and worked backwards, describing each day's events, especially the details of labor and delivery.

When dinner came, we paused and ate, appreciating that someone else would wash the dishes. It was liberating and scary to be away from the telephone—the hospital didn't know where we were. But Cade looked good, she really did. "I hate the thought of suing," I said.

"Hey, I do too," Fred said.

"Your mom says we should."

"If it's the right thing to do, we'll do it. And what about insurance?" Fred said. "What if no one will cover her?"

"True." I hated the thought of court, the violation of privacy it entailed. After my parents got divorced, they fought about money. The last resort, my mother said, would be to take my father to court. I pictured his defensive, chest-thrusting posture. Cecily and I would go, too, and I imagined us bowing our heads on the witness stand as we talked about how when my bicycle got wrecked in a car accident the insurance money had to be used for the electric bill. "How low did my blood pressure drop?" I asked Fred.

"72 over 40," he said, and we wrote some more.

This was the first writing I did about Cade's birth, and I had no idea how much writing would follow, spiral notebooks full of recollections in blue ink. There would be notes scribbled at the tops of pages—details remembered late, details to remember for the pages to come—and research notes from medical books and articles, a timeline gleaned from hospital records. What was the record for? I came to recognize it as the only way through, the channel for me from past to present. The writing felt like clear water, with no pretensions, no particular style compared to the poetry I wrote. Walk onstage with your voice at its highest level, a poetry teacher used to advise. Not here. Here I wanted to claim my observations, and know myself as alive in the time between the beginning of labor and the ending of being the mother of a healthy child. I wanted to posit a history which felt as crucial to me as the end result. I couldn't feel the present without examining this past; unlike other events in my life, it couldn't be absorbed without explication. I don't know why this is so. Maybe I could absorb anything rotten that happened to me, but not to a child of mine. The strangeness of watching a child suffer, a child who was both me and not-me in her infancy, may have led me to suppress myself as I fixed my gaze on her. Later, as she recovered, I could recover a muted self.

Fred wrote a story called "Baby Girl," a fictional story with some of the events of this account heightened, compressed, rear-ranged. I reviewed each draft with editorial detachment and made suggestions, as we do for each other's work. He read it aloud in Provincetown to a large audience, in which I sat in the front row, a happy and supportive wife. Unexpectedly, as he read, my lungs began to constrict, my throat to tighten, my face to set in a hard neutral mask. I felt each spoken word in my chest. I couldn't bear to hear it, this work which made the pain of our baby's almost-death real—I couldn't sit in public and hear it. I concen-trated on not screaming, and on breathing. *Just breathe.* After, while everyone chatted and drank wine out of plastic cups, I lay on the floor in our apartment and sobbed into the carpet as if it had all happened the day before. No, writing wasn't therapeutic in the patronizing way everyone said it was. Writing was a horror show which made the past live again, like the killer who rises up again behind the couch with the knife, just as the babysitter relaxes. How could we do it? I'll never listen to that story again, I told him. How could we not?

In the evening, we watched Cade as she slept in her bassinet. When she woke she would look at us, like any other baby. I couldn't wait to bring her home, to have her to ourselves. We could stop talking to nurses and being observed by them. Most parents left the hospital 24 hours after delivery—one nurse taught them infant care, and then they took the baby home. In our case, nurse after nurse wanted to watch us change her diaper, lift her up and put her down. After Fred would carefully copy one nurse's method of burping Cade, another would say, "I'd rub her back instead of patting." I was losing patience. *I want to take my baby home now,* I thought fiercely.

"When do you think she'll be hungry again?" I asked the nurse, who had fed her formula in our absence, because none of the breastmilk was defrosted.

"9:30 or so."

"We'll be back in a while then."

We got cups of ice from the dispenser on the maternity ward, next to a room with a refrigerator and a microwave which had a handwritten sign on the door: Food for Maternity Patients Only. I had eaten the regular hospital food, but some people brought their own. The electrician who installed the new heating system in our apartment had brought food for his wife when she had their baby at Bismarck; the Chinese custom is for a mother to eat a special diet for thirty days after giving birth, to restore her strength. A new mother shuffled in slippers on the linoleum. She wore two hospital gowns, like a nightgown and bathrobe, and held one hand to the small of her back. Standing in the maternity ward hallway, I felt reluctant to leave. When we took Cade home on Saturday, the crisis would have passed, with all the attention a crisis garners from both the hospital and people outside. We could cope with crisis. When it was over, when we had our baby home and our life back, we would experience the pain of it, as if only in reliving and retelling could our emotions be truly felt.

Near the nursery were open shelves of clean linen—bedsheets, hospital gowns, cribsheets, and baby blankets. Around a corner we glimpsed a large room with one lamp on, a computer on a desk, and a cot, a jacket thrown over a chair. Someone sat at the desk with an open file folder. Maybe Dr. Hanover sat at this desk after his nursery visits, scrawling notes on lined paper. We took sheets to make up our bed on the floor.

"I cannot believe she got formula again," Fred said.

"All our stupid jars of milk."

"What do you have to do," Fred said. "To defrost it?"

"Hold it under hot water? I saw one of the nurses doing that."

As we were arranging the room for sleeping, a security guard knocked. He wrote down our names and gave us clip-on hospital visitor tags. We wore them. We unpacked our pajamas. Then we went and sat with Cade until it was time for feeding. Just this night, and one more night, and then she'd come home.

"Maybe we should go out tomorrow," Fred said.

"I'd like that," I said.

"I'll make a reservation in the morning."

"You guys deserve it," the nurse said.

We took a dozen jars of milk home with us in the morning when we left for rounds. Cade's sleeping basket waited on the trunk by our bed. Our best armchair was set up for breastfeeding, with a box for a footstool, an extra pillow in back. I vacuumed the bedroom and nursery. Fred washed the dishes. We had blankets and bath towels, and a thermometer, and Tylenol drops, and two baby-care books, and a mobile for the crib, stuffed bears clinging to stars. I studied all of Cade's belongings, the brush and comb, the red-and-green Mexican rug, cottonballs, diaper ointment, a china dish—everything couldn't be seen at once, there was too much. I laid out two sleeper suits, one smaller, one bigger, and three blankets, to take to the hospital the next day. Then we went back.

The afternoon nurse's willingness to chat and dispense advice worked well with my anxious energy. It seemed that Cade really would come home the next day. Fred looked at her and touched her arm while Cade gazed placidly up. Her breathing rate was accelerated, but she was tolerating room air very well. She needed rest. The nurse and I leaned on an empty warming bed, while she wrote out advice for us on pieces of notepaper. She said, "You should choose just one person outside the family who can touch her, to limit exposure."

"So everyone else . . ."

"Everyone else can look at her and tell you how beautiful she is," she said with a smile. "But they shouldn't touch her or hold her. Relatives can. And anyone who touches her should wash their hands first, including you. Wash your hands as often as possible."

"What about going outside?"

"Outside is great. But she shouldn't go where there are crowds—too many germs. If you have to take her to the grocery store, go in the morning when no one's there."

Fred looked up. "We live across the street from Golden Gate Park."

"Perfect. I'm writing down about temperature." She held the piece of paper out to me. "At 36.5, add a sweater. At 37.2, take something off. Easy, right?"

I said, "What else have you got?"

"Skin care, diaper rash, signs of illness, and no honey for a year—babies can't process honey, the organisms in it that cause botulism. There's speculation that some crib deaths are really due to honey."

"My god." I read the list of signs of illness.

"Remember, call us day or night with questions. We know your baby." She wagged her pen at us. "And if anyone gives you a hard time about being protective of your baby, you tell them doctor's orders, okay?"

I stared at her.

She smiled. "People will want to pass a baby around the room. Or they won't understand why you can't bring her over to their house."

"We shouldn't do that?"

"More germs. It's up to you. I wouldn't want to see this baby get pneumonia."

Dr. Hanover came in and leaned against the sink. "So we're really taking her home?" I said.

"That's what we expect." He scratched his chin. "We'll be watching her feedings and breath rate. She has made amazing progress. We didn't anticipate such a fast recovery."

"Neither did we," Fred said.

"I'll see you in my office Thursday?" Dr. Hanover said.

"Thursday," Fred said. I hadn't kept track of days. Cade was born on a Tuesday, but I persisted in thinking she was born on a Saturday, because her birth felt like we'd come to the end, a near-dead stop before the tentative revival of a Sunday morning.

"Time for feeding," the nurse said. "We could try it in a parents' room this time."

"Out of the nursery?" I smoothed my yellow gown nervously.

"She's all yours tomorrow, Mom. No nurses, no doctors." She turned Cade's bed gently and wheeled her into the anteroom, through it, and into the hall. We followed behind, not bothering to ungown. She was out of the nursery. We turned into the room, and there was our baby, still in a hospital bassinet, but surrounded by ordinary furniture. I sat on the couch and got ready. The baby latched on without opening her eyes. "I'll come back in a while," the nurse whispered.

Fred sat next to me. "She's hungry."

I nodded, afraid that the sound or movement would make her fall off. After a while I switched to the other breast, and that worked, she kept on nursing. We were all alone together in the quiet room. Cade fell asleep after a few minutes, and we carefully placed her on her side in the bassinet, a rolled up blanket at her back for support. We covered her with a white flannel blanket and tucked it in. We might have lingered over this gesture, except that the nursery seemed to exert a strong magnetic pull. What if something were wrong? Fred wheeled her back to the nursery so she could be hooked up to the heart monitor. In 24 hours, we'd be bringing her into our monitorless home.

It was as if we'd had a baby in slow motion. All of my experiences and emotions were stretched out and articulated over hours and days instead of bundled into minutes. I had a baby and six days later I held her. I had a baby and nursed her seven days later. Eight days later she held my finger. Nine days later we sat on the couch together. Ten days later we would bring her home. "There were lights soft as milk striking/Across the large, distant delay," the poet David St. John wrote, and an image of a small valley came to mind, a valley we'd lived on one side of in Vence, in a cold apartment just outside the town walls. At night, blue-white streetlamps came on to light the curving road on the other side of the valley, which appeared so close to us. But when we drove, winding down our hillside, across, and up, it took a long time to get there. A church with a pink crumbling facade was there, flanked by umbrella pines, and a restaurant with a yellow velvet bar where we spent too much money on drinks one night. You had to stifle your impatience, because everything was pretty over there; you would touch the open roses with your hand.

It was time for Cade's first bath. My hands seemed too calloused to feel the delicacy of her skin. We placed her in the inch of water in the tub, propping her against the slanted back. She cried her soft ragged cries and turned red in the face. She cried until the nurse lifted her out and wrapped her in a towel. We put a clean diaper on. We brushed her damp hair, which was lighter brown after a shampoo. We swabbed her umbilicus and pulled a white long-sleeved t-shirt over her head. "Be sure to reach into that sleeve and get all five fingers," the nurse said. "I've seen babies get their fingers broken." I reached in and grasped her fingers, and bunched them to pull through the sleeve, like closing a starfish; Fred did the other sleeve. The nurse put a pink-and-blue striped knit cap on the baby, which matched Cade's dark blue eyes and pink bow-shaped mouth. She resembled the baby who'd slept in my room on the maternity ward, in a hospital-issue cap, t-shirt and blanket. As she approached normalcy, I think I wished to tell myself that the damage was being undone, bit by bit.

We rolled her back through the middle nursery room, to her spot on the other end. "It seems empty now," I commented as we walked through.

"We're moving to the new nursery in a week," the nurse said. "They're not transferring any babies here at the moment." Fewer nurses were on the unit, and just two babies in the middle nursery room, and Baby Ashley next to Cade. We realized we'd been watching pieces of equipment get wheeled out over the past few days.

"Will the new nursery be bigger?" I said.

"Yes, thank god."

"It must be nice to be less busy here," Fred said.

"You bet. Last week was frantic." I knew almost nothing about what normalcy meant for the ICN, or what a nurse's work involved. She picked up her clipboard. "What's the schedule?"

"We were thinking of going out to dinner," I said.

"Okay. Can you feed her before you go?"

"Of course."

"Good. And you're spending the night?"

"No," I said uncomfortably. "Nina said the rooms are booked, and parents don't usually stay the last night."

"Okay, so the nurse will give her bottles." She smiled briefly and looked at her clipboard. She thought we should be staying.

In the evening, after I'd nursed Cade, we went out to a French restaurant for an early dinner. We'd made a reservation for nine, the only time available, but at six o'clock I was too tired to wait. Fred doubleparked while I conferred with the maitre'd—I was prepared to say I'd just had a baby, and . . . I'm not sure what else. But the man required no explanation, he granted us a small table near the kitchen.

I wore a black dress, and earrings. The waiters carried platters of lamb chops arranged into crowns, shrimp arrayed like flowers. Tiny vegetables glistened, and pale sauces trailed in unintelligible script around the food. The restaurant was noisy and festive by seven o'clock. People ordered cocktails, appetizers, wine. They weren't especially dressed up, as if this were usual for them. At the table we did our best not to lapse into silence, trying to match the easy conversations all around us. I could only have a few sips of wine, since I was breastfeeding, and it was hard to relax into the mood of the room. We were tired and yet awake, hungry and yet stunned by the elaborate food. Finally the waiter brought a two-tiered dish of assorted cookies and we ate a few of them and left.

We returned to the hospital, self-conscious in our dressy clothes. I carried a black purse instead of a canvas bag; my shoes clicked on the hall tiles. A rush of nostalgia, for my own life or possibly a life I'd seen on television, overcame me: the image of parents in evening clothes, perfumed and whispering, tiptoeing up a flagstone path to their house where a baby slept. We walked down a fluorescent hospital hall. We would say, "How is she?" to a nurse, not a babysitter. But the whole distortion of the scene made me want to laugh because everything would be fine; after all, the scene was still true. I wore perfume, Fred whispered in my ear, and our baby lay sleeping down this hallway, in a dimly lit room. We had a baby.

Cade slept tightly swaddled, in a knit cap. The bassinet was tilted up at the head for easier breathing.

"She's coming home tomorrow," I said. We looked at her, sleeping on her side, her mouth slightly open. Her nose was so molded, so complete; I wanted to touch it. People could say she looked like me or Fred, and we all liked to speculate on whose chin or mouth or nose she had. But what really amazed us was how unlike us she was—Cade looked like herself.

"No one can believe it," the nurse said. "How well she's done."

"*Last* Friday night," I said. "We didn't know what would happen."

"It was touch and go," she said. "Of course she wouldn't be leaving us so soon if it weren't for your involvement."

"Really?" I said.

"Sure. It's a factor we consider, how involved the parents are."

I sat on the stool and looked at Cade. How long would they have kept her? I felt upset that they had been watching us so closely, that our behavior could affect her discharge date unbeknownst to us. I'd thought discharge was determined by her medical condition. But I felt proud of us all, parents and grandparents, for passing their tests. I was frightened, too—was Cade ready to come home? Should she stay in the hospital longer? I thought of other parents—were other parents less involved? Did they care less about their babies? Or did they live farther away from the hospital, did they have other children, did they have to go to work, were their babies in the hospital for weeks or months?

"Are you ready to take her home?" the nurse asked.

"Definitely ready," Fred said.

She wrote in her notes that we'd stated we were ready for our daughter's discharge from the nursery.

In the morning we packed the diaper bag with baby clothes, two blankets, a soft rattle, a pacifier. I was efficient and yet nervous, adding two carseat head supports, four diapers, and an extra cotton cap to the bag before I was done. We visited Cade and I nursed her, and then we walked down the hill from the hospital to the medical office building for the Saturday morning infant and child CPR class. We'd suggested that we take the class, which had somehow been transformed into a requirement for Cade's discharge. In the deserted building we took the elevator to an upper floor and found the classroom, a carpeted conference room with tables surrounded by chairs. We sat down. Other people came in and found seats. I took out a notepad and pen and laid them on the table. I worried that my breasts would leak milk, that I wouldn't be able to sit comfortably in the chair for three hours. Did I look like I'd just had a baby, did I look fat?

A team of instructors lined up at the front of the room. They were dressed in bright official t-shirts and casual pants, and as they stood with hands clasped behind their backs and introduced themselves their bodies looked seamless, taut, even airfilled. We'd spent too many hours in the nursery; reality looked garish. The instructors had white teeth and loud voices, and worked as a family first aid and CPR roadshow, traveling up and down the peninsula in a van, doing gigs at hospitals and offices. They had charts, slides, and peach-colored rubber baby and child dummies. After handing out booklets, they gave a slide show about accidents in the home. It was a relief to sit in the dark and watch colored pictures go by.

The slides laboriously proceeded through emergency instructions—one slide showed only a telephone and the numbers 911 above it—and then depicted a harrowing array of household dangers. A woman held a baby in her lap and lifted a mug of coffee to her mouth. An instructor said, "In my work as a paramedic, I have seen so many burns. And tea is even worse than coffee because of the tannins. Be extremely aware of children near hot beverages, and never drink one with a child on your lap." Pot handles had to be turned inward on the stove; extension cords were not to be overloaded. Carpet had to be tacked down, gates put up, windows prevented from opening too far. (We lived on the fourth floor!) Household poisons such as detergent and glue, liquor and aspirin, and eye makeup, had to be discarded or stored in high, locked cabinets. Toys had to be carefully examined for detachable parts—the plastic eyes on teddy bears could be chewed off and choked on. The show concluded with pictures of safety devices: outlet covers, cabinet latches, smoke detectors, a thermometer for checking bathwater. How could a baby hope to survive?

The instructors took questions from the floor. A man asked about window latches. A woman said her sister had just had a baby, and she'd be babysitting sometimes, and could they talk about SIDS. They could, one of the instructors said, but not much was known, except that most deaths occurred between twelve and eight a.m. Sleeping positions seemed to be a factor—babies should sleep on their stomachs.

"I heard the side is better," a woman said.

"Oh really," an instructor said dismissively. "I hadn't heard that."

"The nurses in intensive care," I found myself saying, "put babies on their sides." My face was hot. "A new study by the Russians. They roll up a blanket and put it behind the baby's back for support." What was I doing talking, and mentioning intensive care?

"Now we'll go through CPR procedure," an instructor said. "It's not like the emergency shows on TV, where the victim starts breathing all of a sudden. Most victims don't come back."

We were granted a 15-minute break. A security guard unlocked the vending machine room next door and I bought juice.

A woman said to me, "You have a baby in intensive care?"

"Yes. But she's coming home today."

"Was she premature?"

"No," I said. "She had meconium aspiration syndrome." I felt very tired, because I saw that I would be telling this story over and over.

"Oh, MAS," the woman said. "I know a couple of kids who had it."

"Are they okay now?"

"Sure. The one who had it worse, he's three now, gets colds a lot, but otherwise he's great."

"Was he on a respirator?"

"No. Oxygen hood. Yours?"

"Respirator for eight days." Did I somehow enjoy the fact that my baby had been sicker? Was this a war story?

"Mmm." She shook her head. "I'll tell you something, though. Those kids, they're both so intense, they can really focus."

I didn't know how to respond so I said, "That's great." Focus—what the hell was that? I was feeling sarcastic. I was feeling odd, the way I did when I'd been shut up in a room reading all day and then had to go to the grocery store—I'd feel exposed and jumpy, regarding my own hand, as I laid items on the conveyor belt, as an alien limb. How pink it looked, embracing the shiny green box with red lettering!

We were all supposed to practice rescue breathing and CPR on a baby dummy and a child dummy. Fred and I headed for the baby dummy at the front of the room. We were supposed to enact an emergency and our response. I picked up the rubber dummy and looked, listened with my ear to its chest, and felt, with my face close to its face, my first two fingers on its neck, then on the upper arm for the brachial pulse.

"She's not breathing," I said, as if in a play, the kind we staged as children, with a concept but no script. I put my mouth over the dummy's nose and mouth and breathed, gently. I straightened up and pointed at Fred. "Call 911," I said. "I think she's choked on something." A grape, I thought. I looked into the shallow pink cavity. "There's nothing in the mouth," I said. "What do I do?"

"On your arm," the instructor said. I maneuvered the dummy onto my forearm, stomach down, my hand gripping its chin. I lowered its head. I struck the dummy on the back with the heel of my hand, between where shoulderblades would be.

"Harder," the instructor said, and I hit harder, three more times.

"I think something came out," I said.

"Nothing came out," the instructor said.

"Fine," I said, and turned the dummy over so it faced me. "I check for breathing." I held my cheek near the mouth and nose and looked out the corner of my eye at the instructor.

"Still not breathing," he said. I measured two fingers down from the dummy's nipples and with two fingers I gave four quick thrusts to the sternum.

"There it is," the instructor said. So I laid the dummy down, tilted the head back slightly to open the airway, and gave two breaths.

"Chest didn't rise," the instructor said. "Tighter seal, longer breath." This time I put my hand on the dummy's chest and felt for movement. I breathed longer and the chest rose.

"Check the brachial," the instructor said. I put two fingers on the dummy's inner upper arm and pressed gently. "Is there a pulse?" I said.

He shook his head.

"Five and one for a baby," I said, and while keeping the dummy's head tilted for open airway with one hand, I pressed on the sternum with two fingers, one-two-three-four-five, then gave a breath, then pressed five more times, then breathed.

"The pulse is back," the instructor said. "Very good." I let go of the dummy. He picked it up and wiped the nose and mouth with an alcohol towelette. "Next?"

Fred stepped forward and I could tell he thought he could remember what to do much better than I had. I put a hand on my hip. After hanging around intensive care for ten days, could we really take this pink-dummy-doll business seriously? The ceiling was low in the conference room, the blackboards chalky, the carpet a mustard-and-brown weave, and I was having a 1970's open-pod classroom flashback. Fred took the dummy by the arm and said, "Okay, baby." Then he looked up, utterly blank. I wanted to laugh, a big, joyous human laugh. We were almost free.

"Look, listen, and feel," the instructor said. Fred laid the dummy down on the table, tilted its head back to open the airway, and brought his face down close. He turned and said, with a convincing look of surprise, "She's not breathing." He'd been a child actor. He gave her a breath.

"Get help," the instructor said. Fred pointed at me authoritatively. "Call 911," he said. Then he did all the moves, the back blows, chest thrusts, rescue breathing, pulse checking, with great dexterity, until the instructor decreed that the baby was breathing again.

In the hallway, Fred said, "Let's go get our baby." He jabbed at the elevator button.

"They didn't even check our tests," I said.

"Joke of a class."

"It wasn't so bad, was it?" I loved school.

"Four hours." He banged open the door to the stairway. We hurried down seven flights.

"Do you think they'll really let us have her?" I said.

"I don't know," Fred said. "We might have to give her another bath."

We retrieved the carseat and diaper bag and headed up the hill. We'd almost brought the carseat with us when I'd gone into labor but we'd thought, No, I'll be in the hospital for a day, Fred will go home to shower, and when he comes back he can bring the carseat then. Good planning.

Cade lay awake in her bassinet. Her dark blue eyes moved from side to side as we stood over her, and her closed hands made fitful movements. "She's probably hungry," the nurse said. "You can use a parents' room to change her and feed her if you like. Everything you need is under her bed."

"Thanks." I'd envisioned changing her clothes, strapping her into the carseat, and leaving the hospital. But we'd be here at least an hour now. *That's not important,* I told myself. *Be patient.* Fred wheeled the bassinet down the hall and turned into a room.

"Another hour," I said.

"Take it easy. Now do we change her or feed her first?"

Cade started to cry. "I'd better feed her." I sat on the couch. Fred picked up the baby, holding her wobbly head close, and handed her to me. She took hungry little sucks and then panted. She was getting stronger. My heels lifted off the floor with the pain. "Okay, okay," I said, calming myself.

"Hurts?" Fred said.

"Supposed to go away after a while."

He sat close to me. "We're taking our baby home."

When she'd finished nursing, Fred burped her against his shoulder. I unpacked a soft stretchy suit, white with a pastel print, and held it up. It seemed the right size. I wished it were a brighter color, purple or red, like a banner. Cade was going home.

"If you could change her," Fred said, "I'd go get the car and pull it up to that back door." He laid her in the bassinet.

I changed her diaper and dressed her in the suit and cap. I packed up everything from her cart, the crib card, the music box and puppy and photograph, her hospital clothes, white blankets, a thermometer. The nurse came in. "I brought you a plastic bag. Take that mattress pad, too—it'll just get thrown out." I put it in the bag. Fred came back.

"The carseat's strapped in," he said. "Are we ready?"

"Yes," I said.

"I'll take the baby," Fred said. "And the diaper bag."

"Are you sure?"

"You get that other bag," he said. He slung the diaper bag over his shoulder and gently lifted Cade from the bassinet. He held her against his chest, her head curled into his neck.

"I'll get the door," the nurse said. Fred went first and we followed behind, turning left and left, passing the side of the nursery with covered windows, where the nurses would raise the blinds upon request from one until two in the afternoon, so friends and relatives could see the babies. Cade's bed had been too far across the room, behind too much equipment, to be seen; we'd never told anyone to come look. When we'd taken the labor and delivery tour, two months before, the nurses had raised the blinds so we could see the preemies in their isolettes. I could see one baby from where I stood then—a nurse put a hand through a porthole and soothed the baby by stroking its chest with her finger. How remote the baby had seemed, behind glass, encased in plastic, parts of its body obscured by tubing and tape. I hadn't considered that our baby's life might occur in that room. I turned my eyes from the covered window.

The nurse held the door open as I passed through, and came out behind me. She peered into the backseat of the rental car. "Good carseat," she said. "Take care of that baby."

"We sure will," Fred said. "Thanks."

"Bye, folks." She gave a wave and disappeared behind the door as she pulled it shut. We'd passed the last test. We were out.

Sunlight glared against the pale asphalt. Some gravel and a bottlecap glinted. It was bare out here, and quiet. Fred was painstakingly lowering Cade into her seat. From where we stood, at the top of the hill in back of it, the hospital was a blank pink box, with doors marked No Entry, its brand-new glassy facade invisible. I slid into the car next to Cade. Fred pulled the straps over her head and buckled her in.

He said, "Shall we go home?"

9

"Lungs heal," Dr. Hanover said at our nursery follow-up. "The tissue is regenerative. As for the brain, we'll have to watch her development, but just look at her." He waved a kleenex in the air above her face and her eyes moved. "She's alert. When she gets to be five years old and she doesn't color inside the lines, who can say what caused that?"

We had to make sure she gained weight, since she'd lost half a pound in the hospital. She was to be nursed every two to three hours, though once a night, we could let her go for four hours. We had to protect her from germs; visitors had to wash their hands as soon as they entered the apartment. People who were just getting sick were especially contagious and weren't to be near the baby. We were to avoid unnecessary contact with people, and not take her into stores. He advised us to call right away if she caught a cold, or if we noticed any changes in her breathing.

Some people thought we were overly anxious and protective. We didn't let people hold the baby. We made everyone wash their hands when they came in, whether they were planning to touch her or not. We didn't take her anywhere indoors. The only person who didn't think we were extreme or inappropriately fearful was Fred's sister Betsy, who'd been through neonatal intensive care with Jonathan. After he'd come home, Jonathan had contracted respiratory syncytial virus when he was several months old, and spent a week in pediatric intensive care, where they didn't even change his diapers regularly. The thought of Cade returning to the intensive care nursery was bad enough, but of course she wouldn't be admitted there again—she'd go to a whole new unit, with different procedures and unfamiliar nurses and doctors. At night, I'd wake up and lean over her basket to hear her breathing. I couldn't bear the idea of her suffering more pain, or fear. Whenever someone gave a little laugh when we ordered them to wash their hands, I'd think angrily, *You have a baby in intensive care, and then let's see how you feel about germs.*

New babies slept an average of seventeen hours a day, according to our books, but Cade only slept for seven. When she slept, I slept, developing the skill of falling asleep instantly. For a while Fred stayed up with me during the night feedings to keep me company. We discovered overnight news shows, the minor leagues for anchorpeople, some of whom flirted with each other at the desk. Maybe they figured nobody was watching, or maybe it was part of the concept. The same stories were told, the same clips aired, at 1:00, at 2:00, at 3:30, at 4:52, over and over throughout the night. The baby was content at night. After the first few minutes of nursing, Fred and I could talk. In the daytime we occasionally felt confined by our apartment, and overly tired, but at night we felt comforted by being together, sealed in a warm room against the cold darkness outside. Tiredness was natural at three a.m., nothing to fight against. I'd look out the window and see lit windows on our street, and feel a kinship with the other night wakers, or early risers, out there. My mother told me she could remember feeding me and watching the sun come up as she sat utterly glazed with exhaustion. In our apartment the sun rose at the back, lighting up the kitchen first and then the front bedroom. At a certain hour, outside the kitchen window, the dark blue sky turned to yellow and the gray tops of the eucalyptus trees in the park became green, while out front the yellow clamshell of the lit gas station sign still glowed against black.

An audiologist, John Ballardi, taped electrodes all over the baby's head to measure brain waves. He carefully secured each electrode while Cade cried and cried.

"I'm really sorry, you guys," he said, holding out a piece of tape. "She just has so much hair." Fred held her on his lap as the audiologist stood over her with a handful of wires. He kept pushing tortoise-shell glasses back up on his nose.

"The test only takes thirty minutes," he said. "But the thing is, you guys, she has to be lying quietly. Do you think she'll do that?"

We looked at her doubtfully. Brightly colored wires sprouted all over her head. She'd just been changed and fed, so all we could do was try to calm her somehow.

"Do you think she'll sleep?" the audiologist said, and Fred laughed. "Let's get her into position." He directed us so that Cade lay on her back on Fred's lap, her head at his knees. I sat pulled up close to Fred's chair, with my hands at Cade's head so I could hold the rigid plastic tubing which had to be positioned in her ear and held still. Dr. Ballardi would sound certain tones in her ear and record brainwaves. The test took three hours because Cade cried so much; Fred and I traded positions, rocked her on our knees, and sang a song of ours she liked that went: Who's the sweet potato, the sweetest little potato, who's the sweet potato that we love. We hadn't yet sung it in public.

"You guys have been through so much," Dr. Ballardi said.

"You must be so tired. And colic, too, oh you guys, I don't know. Our baby girl is just getting over colic."

"How old is she?" I asked.

"Six months."

"Six months," Fred said grimly. "The books say three months."

"The books, you guys. The books make it sound like colic just goes away one day, but it doesn't. It's been a process. My wife says we have a high-need baby."

"High-need," I said. "I like that."

"Yeah, some people might say difficult, but we say high-need. My wife's home full time with her; she was working part time, but not anymore. You guys, she's quiet, should we try?"

When he'd finished the first set of tones, he swiveled his desk monitor so we could see the blue brain waves. "Peaks and valleys," he said. "That's a good response. The more the waves look like mountains, the better it is. Now I'll repeat the series so we know it's not random. Are you guys in position?"

His calmness and litany of "you guys" were very soothing. Our ability to maintain a conversation while the baby cried testified to his long experience, and our short one, with colic. So the baby screamed inconsolably, so what? The concept of a high-need baby was interesting; everything could go perfectly in childbirth and yet you could still have to quit a part-time job because your baby needed you to be home.

"Do you see all the babies from the ICN?" I asked.

"I see a lot, you guys. Oh the parents are so tired, so tired. But your baby looks great, just great."

The opthalmologist, who thought Cade looked fine, too, performed a harrowing test using spring-clips to keep the baby's eyelids wide open. It looked exactly like the torture scene from "Clockwork Orange," which I could barely stand to watch. I had had no idea, when watching the movie, that those clips were a bona fide piece of medical equipment. Cade turned purple with hysteria, but then that wasn't unusual. She could tolerate very little stimulation. Her stuffed-bear mobile made her cry after a few minutes. The black-and-white visual stimulation mobile we bought made her cry after a few seconds. If we took a walk and had visitors in the same day, she cried longer and more continuously at night. Sometimes she would be calm when friends came over to see us, but as soon as they left she'd vomit. Music made her cry, except for one lullaby tape that helped her fall asleep, which we played over and over throughout the night, waking to flip the tape, slam it into its slot, and listen to the artificially slowed and sweetened songs. Loud voices made her cry, and laughter especially upset her. She liked our voices, when we talked quietly or sang to her. She liked the sound of the hairdryer and vacuum cleaner, and we propped the hairdryer next to the nursing chair so I could calm her enough for breastfeeding. Because her nose was chronically stuffed up, we tried different nursing positions, and Fred and I aspirated her nose frequently with a rubber bulb. The suctioning took time, and soothing her after took time, since she usually hyperventilated. "Take her," I'd say to Fred, and he'd carry her until she was breathing well enough to nurse again. She liked to be held, and often we held her almost all day long.

When Cade had been home for three weeks, we went to see an attorney. We took a taxi downtown, to a marble-lobbied building on California Street. A framed photograph of the attorney's wife and four children sat on the bookshelf behind his desk, which was impressively large, as was the view of the city and the Golden Gate bridge from his window. Rollins appeared to be in his early forties, and wore unstylish metal-framed glasses. He wore a thick wedding ring. He looked like a practical man.

He asked us to tell the story of labor and delivery. He did

not seem sympathetic or unsympathetic. We described labor, my blood pressure drop, the evidence of fetal distress, Dr. Greg's question of, "What do I do now?" We detailed how the baby was put on my chest, then taken away by the nurse, how Fred had to find the light switch, how there was no one to help, no equipment ready. We included the neonatologist's question about proceeding with a vaginal delivery, Becca's mention that the intensive care respiratory team was not put on alert. We had no problem with the intensive care nursery, we emphasized, but perhaps the labor and delivery team had not performed well. All the articles we'd read were prefaced with the comment that meconium aspiration was largely preventable.

"We'll have our physician check into that." He peered over the desk at the baby. I turned her around to face him. "She looks good now." He kept writing in roundish script.

Fred leaned over to me and said in a low voice, "I wonder if Greg will be reprimanded."

"I don't know," I whispered.

"Do you think she'll feel it, that she did something wrong?"

"Why don't you ask him," I said, not looking up at the lawyer.

"I don't think it's appropriate." He straightened up in his chair.

Rollins put down his pen and leaned back. "We have the burden of proving that better intervention could have made a difference. She has until she's eight years old to sue. If she's fine, there won't be any finding of negligence for damage. From what I see now, you couldn't win enough on a pain and suffering case to make back the legal fees."

"Her pain and suffering?" I asked.

"Yours, too," he said. "And mental anguish. But it's not enough. Should she develop problems later on, she could sue."

"We're not interested in suing," I said, "just for the sake of it.

But if she has medical expenses because of what happened, or if she can't get health insurance, then we don't think it should cost us." I felt myself becoming defensive. We're not litigious people, I kept thinking. We don't want to go to court, relive the experience again and again.

"If she's healthy, she'll probably become insurable again. And your added costs for insurance won't be enough to cover a law-suit." He explained that if we signed a standard contingency con-tract, he could begin investigating. Rollins would get 40% of any damage award up to $50,000, 33% of the next $50,000, and 15% of the rest. At least we didn't have to pay him anything up front.

Fred gave a barely perceptible shrug. "Let's do it."

I never thought I'd have to see an attorney. I never thought I'd have to see a personal injury attorney. There was something distasteful about seeking money for pain and suffering—wasn't pain and suffering a part of life? I didn't want to assume the attitude of a child who stamped its little foot and screamed, It's not fair! I didn't want to be a complainer; I'd much rather tell a happy childbirth story than the one I'd just told Rollins. I knew obstetricians were leaving the practice because of the cost of mal-practice insurance; I knew childbirth had its risks and that people who'd had less-than-perfect experiences often felt a need to cast blame. C-sections were sometimes performed on the women who wanted them least, those who'd taken childbirth preparation classes, because these educated women were the very ones most likely to sue over an undesirable outcome. They couldn't sue over a cesarean, but they could sue over a baby damaged by fetal dis-tress. Was I one of these women, unable to accept the potential for problems in childbirth? But the thought that weighed on me most was that this baby could suffer because of the hospital's mistakes, and no one would be held responsible, as long as she was fine in the end.

In time, we received a note from Mr. Rollins, explaining that the staff doctor did not see any indication of negligence on the part of Bismarck. He recommended that we wait several years to see how Cade did; if serious problems developed, a neonatologist would review the records. The staff doctor had found that the fetal monitor didn't indicate distress severe or continuous enough to warrant a cesarean delivery. The initial resuscitation and care in the ICN conformed to relevant standards. There was "very little basis in these records for seriously criticizing the care either Rhett or her baby received." In his conclusion he noted that "severe meconium aspiration syndrome can be fatal in a high percentage of infants, and those surviving may exhibit neurological and other problems associated with hypoxia." Pediatric visits, though, showed no "clinical abnormalities"; vision and hearing tests revealed no "gross abnormalities."

"So far," he finished, "we have no records suggesting that Cade suffered any injury in association with meconium aspiration syndrome."

The day we received the birth certificate, we were excited. We picked it up at a grilled window in a cold hallway, the same window that issued death certificates. "Certificate of Live Birth" it said at the top, "State of California." Typed into numbered boxes were her name, date and time of birth, the hospital address, our names and birthdates, and the birth attendant's name, G. Greg. In box number 13B, for license number, the word "pending" was typed.

"Pending, what does that mean?" I asked. We stared at the word.

"She doesn't have a license?"

"That was in July," I said. "Maybe she has one now."

I called the State of California Medical Board to verify Gail Greg's license; she didn't have one. The woman advised me to call

Bismarck for the exact spelling of her name, and her license number. "That's your right, you had your baby there." She thought for a moment. "Maybe she uses a different name, hyphenated or married. If she works at Bismarck, she must be licensed. Call us back when you get the spelling."

I called Patient Relations at Bismarck and left a message on the voice mail. I called Medical Legal Correspondence and talked to a Julie, who said she didn't have Gail Greg's name in her directory. She transferred me to the Bismarck operator, who said, "Oh yes, she's an intern," and transferred me to Medical Education. I asked the woman at Medical Education how it was that Gail Greg didn't have a license, and she said, "I'm not authorized to release that information."

"She delivered my baby," I said. "According to the state medical board, I have a right to know."

"Let me explain licensure to you," she said impatiently. "By the beginning of the third year, residents are required to have a license. First-year residents are not licensed yet; they aren't required to obtain one until the end of the second year. She's only a first-year resident."

"Thank you," I said, and hung up. Medical school ended in May or June, I thought. If she was a first-year resident now, in March, then she had started her residency last June or July. When she delivered our baby at the end of July, she'd only been working for a few weeks. In fact, interns, as first-year residents are called, did arrive fresh from medical school in July. The pediatrician Perri Klass, writing about her residency experience in a labor and delivery unit, noted that during July, when interns started practicing what they'd learned, nurses occasionally needed to use their experience to protect their patients.

I called the state medical board again. "Are there state laws governing interns delivering babies?"

"No," the woman said. "There are no state regulations. Your hospital should be able to answer questions regarding guidelines for intern practice."

I called the Bismarck information number, and the operator said they had no intern program office, no one specifically in charge of intern guidelines; maybe the Health Plan office could help me. The Health Plan office existed as a resource for people who had questions about their insurance coverage, and had nothing to do with hospital staff or administration. I didn't feel like telling the Health Plan woman who I was, and experienced a brief thrill at going undercover. I said, "I'm considering switching to Bismarck from another insurance plan, and I'm concerned about having a baby there, since it's a teaching hospital. Would it ever happen that an intern would deliver my baby?"

"No," the woman said. "It's usually a physician."

"Usually? Could it be an intern?"

"No. It would be a licensed physician."

Deflated, I set down the phone. If it wasn't a usual or acceptable practice, then why did an intern deliver our baby? Had there been an emergency in another labor room that evening?

A woman from Patient Relations returned my call. I asked how Labor and Delivery worked at Bismarck. "A team of doctors delivers babies," she said. "The number of doctors depends on the circumstances of the birth."

"Would a doctor ever deliver a baby alone?" I asked. "Or an intern?"

"No," she said. "I don't know specifics, but I know they don't work alone."

"How can I find out specifics?"

"You could call your OB," she said. "Your doctor could give you specifics."

Finally, it was up to my obstetrician, who had never said more than two sentences to me in response to any question, to explain how it happened that a brand new intern had delivered our baby without help. I couldn't imagine that she would criticize her colleagues, or the administration of the labor and delivery unit, to an inquisitive patient. I didn't call her.

I did call Blue Cross of California to see if we could enroll Cade; was she uninsurable?

My baby had been diagnosed with meconium aspiration syndrome and persistent pulmonary hypertension, I told the agent, and I wondered if she could be enrolled, with or without a preexisting condition clause. She put me on hold while she checked with an underwriter. She came back on. "Those conditions are cause for denial of enrollment."

"They won't exclude those conditions as preexisting?"

"No. Straight denial."

"Forever?"

"I asked that," she said. "No matter how long ago the diagnosis, the current guideline is denial."

It was exhausting to be angry. I could feel angry at Gail Greg, as I had a right to—she should have looked at the baby more carefully, she should have been more anxious, asked questions, requested assistance. According to Perri Klass, it's the overconfident intern who can do the most damage. I could be angry at the supervising obstetrician of record, whom I'd never seen, for choosing not to be in the room at delivery, or angry at the hospital for understaffing the labor and delivery unit. I could wonder if the labor nurse should have been more assertive; she told me I could make it through without anesthesia, but she didn't ask anyone to check my dilatation before they administered the epidural. She knew the baby's heart rate was problematic, and she massaged my belly, saying that would help; maybe she should have done something else. I could be angry at fate, or, and it always ended up here, angry at myself for requesting anesthesia. What was the anger for? It was for my baby's suffering. Did it help her? Maybe, when it drove me to protect her. Mostly, it was better put away.

When Cade was nine months old, I noticed some odd upper-body movements, like shudders, but I didn't mention them to the developmental nurse, who visited once a month. I hadn't even mentioned them to Fred, and I'd hardly mentioned them to myself, because I didn't want to see them. *Maybe I'm imagining them,* I thought. Cade had learned to sit up only recently. Maybe she got off balance for a second and it startled her, or maybe she was cold. One day I took her to the playground, sat her down in the sand and gave her nesting cups and a shovel. As we played together I saw her torso shudder and then her right arm lift and wave sinuously. It was as if a spirit had traveled through her body and then her arm and escaped through the fingertips of her right hand, into the air. The shudder traveled slowly, more slowly than the little tremors I'd seen at home, which I suddenly realized were just like this. Here she sat in the sand on a sunny afternoon—she wasn't off balance, wasn't cold.

At home, I read about cerebral palsy again. Until the late nineteenth century, children with cerebral palsy were institutionalized and left untreated. John Little, a British physician, was the first to study the causes and to classify the different motor disorders described by the term. According to the classification section, Cade's movement would be called a shudder, and would fall under athetosis, which was especially common after neonatal asphyxia. I didn't know. Certainly she was doing the appropriate developmental things, like sitting up and eating finger foods. Cade didn't seem floppy, or stiff. She was alert and curious. Fred wasn't sure if he'd noticed any shudders. *Maybe they weren't shudders,* I thought again. Babies were bound to make funny movements as they learned how to sit and stand.

Her pediatrician suggested that we keep a notebook of her shuddering episodes. Some days there seemed to be no shudders, and other days there were too many to record. It was hard to account for the phases of denial and worry I experienced, hard to decide whether these periods correlated with periods of no abnormal movement and periods of many tremors. What was real? Did I see that shudder or not? What was normal? Was she adjusting her position, moving her shoulder? What was meaningful? Maybe the movements would decrease or go away, maybe they would become more pronounced.

I most often saw the shudders when Cade sat on the floor and I read books to her. She would look fixedly at the book and sit very still, and it would happen, an uneven shrug of the shoulders or a hunching. Sometimes her shoulders and chest moved from side to side, as if undulating to an invisible current. It would be over in a second, and then she'd just be sitting still again. Sometimes she would shrug her shoulders high, as if she were doing exercises, and her shoulders would stay hunched up until I touched them—maybe she would have relaxed on her own if I'd waited longer. When it happened I couldn't breathe; I would touch her shoulder and say, It's okay, honey. Did looking at books make her tense? Cade seemed to love looking at books, and was increasingly attracted to them instead of toys. She loved flinging books off a bookshelf, and going through her basket of books on the floor, flipping through each one and then throwing it aside. Maybe the shudders happened more in the late afternoon, when she was tired. The hour before her dinner seemed to be the worst. On a couple of days it happened so much I was almost in tears. She was holding out one book after another to be read aloud, but she'd only let me read two or three pages, and then she'd hold up the next selection, and it kept happening, the shoulders hunching up. I couldn't cry. I couldn't let her know I was upset or it would make her more tense; emotional stress was thought to increase the involuntary movements of cerebral palsy.

Then days would go by when I saw nothing, and I would doubt that the odd little movements ever existed. Surely I was an alarmist, think of how many babies were born prematurely—they were all at risk, too, and yet most turned out fine. When we mentioned the shudders to our friends with a baby, they said, "Every kid has something. Ours used to grunt when she went to the bathroom." When we mentioned it to friends without a baby, one said, "I shudder all the time."

"When I'm cold," the other said.

"Or for no reason at all." And they both shuddered, to demonstrate. Maybe people thought we were silly to worry, or wanted to say only cheerful things. Cade *did* look fine. I started to feel like a pessimistic, brooding person when I mentioned it, and resolved not to talk about it anymore.

When we finished our summer teaching in Iowa and had more time, I spent an afternoon at the UCSF medical center library reading about cerebral palsy. One book illustrated the syndrome with black-and-white photographs labeled "Abnormal" or "Normal," showing infants and toddlers in various positions. The babies and small children in the "Abnormal" pictures were as lovely and intelligent-looking as the "Normal" ones, which surprised me. In a couple of cases the abnormal photos showed a child who was exceptionally thin or appeared too infantile in posture for its age. But the differences between normal and abnormal seemed subtle—I needed the labels to tell them apart. Some of the postures in abnormal photos resembled Cade, especially one of a child asleep on her stomach, with her arms and legs tucked under and her rear end high in the air. "Abnormal sleeping position," the caption said, "with weight resting on the head." Cade always fell asleep like that. Another photo caught my eye, of a baby being pulled up by his arms and letting his head flop back. Cade could hold her head straight when she was pulled—the developmental nurse had tested for that—but lately she was letting it flop, which I assumed was a game for her, since she loved looking at things upside-down; but who could tell?

Farther on in the book were photos of children aged four to six, and I could tell which postures were abnormal without the labels. There was a profile shot of a boy standing, with his right knee bent slightly so that only the toes of his foot touched the floor, and his right wrist bent so that the hand curved inward toward the arm. I remembered seeing children like that when I was in kindergarten and elementary school. The tiny abnormalities in babies and toddlers became pronounced as they got older. I flipped back to see the babies again and noticed that in some photos, therapists worked with the babies, showing them how to roll over properly, how to sit more easily, how to balance better. A lot of the babies could do the appropriate developmental things, but not in the best, most normal way.

I skimmed through other books and copied helpful pages. Early signs of cerebral palsy included unusual stiffness in the infant's arms and legs. No, I thought, she's not stiff, but then the stiffness was described as especially evident when changing diapers. Her legs sometimes did stiffen up when we changed her— we said, Relax, and pressed gently on her legs so she would release them. Other symptoms, such as irritability, poor sleep habits, lack of reaction to loud noise, and floppiness didn't apply. Most children were diagnosed by age two, almost all by age four. Athetosis, which I thought described Cade's kind of involuntary movement, was not often seen before babies were eighteen months old. Large motor skills would present less of a problem than small motor skills—the child with athetoid cerebral palsy might be able to walk but would have difficulty picking up a pencil. The child would appear to be slightly clumsy. Or there was spasticity, in which the muscles tended to tighten up, or a mixed type, of spasticity and athetosis. I couldn't possibly diagnose my child, could I? According to the books, physicians needed to make multiple examinations before determining if there was a problem.

The material overwhelmed me, some of it too technical to be wholly understandable. As I struggled with the journal articles, I began to feel like a hysteric, doing this research while I had a perfectly beautiful baby at home. I was spending one of the rare afternoons we had a babysitter reading disturbing articles. Did I want Cade to have a problem? Was I looking for abnormality? I couldn't get over what had happened to my baby. Surely this was a form of grief, searching for a physical manifestation to justify my anxiety. The grief should be acknowledged, felt, and dismissed. It was lonely, being so upset almost a year after the fact, especially when nothing seemed to be wrong to anyone but me. Cade hadn't died, she was lovely and sweet. What was lost, in the end?

I sat with Cade at the playground, in an informal circle of mothers and babies. Our babies played in the sand with a pile of toys, and the mothers asked each other how old the babies were, and who was walking and teething and sleeping through the night. We got on the subject of labor, and all five of us had had epidurals. One mother said, "It was great for pain, but I had the hardest time pushing. Did you?"

"They had to stop the epidural because my blood pressure dropped," I said. "So it was all worn off when I pushed."

"I could push all right, but I had a tear, and that was the worst," another mother said.

"A tear," someone said with a shiver.

"I could barely walk," the woman said.

"Was your baby okay?" someone asked me.

"She had meconium aspiration, so she was on a respirator, but she's fine now," I said, wanting both to tell my story and not tell it. I wished I had a better story, could be the mother who said, "I was in labor for 29 hours," and got horrified, sympathetic looks.

"When I got to twenty hours," that mother said. "I was feeling so bad, I said to the nurse, Honey, bring on that epidural. I'm not suffering no more." Everybody laughed at that.

A woman standing nearby on the grass called out to me, "Did you say your baby was in intensive care?"

"Yes." I picked up Cade and walked over.

"Mine was too. This is Sam." She pointed to a chubby baby sitting on the grass. "He's a year now." I put Cade down next to Sam and sat on the grass. Another woman sat near us, with seven-month-old Leo on her lap. The woman who'd called to me told me that Sam had been taken away from her at delivery, because he wasn't breathing well, and put in intensive care under an oxygen hood. He'd had pneumonia.

"Was it terrible for you when you brought the baby home?" she said. "I mean, it was terrible when he was in the hospital, but it was still bad when he came home. We were so tired, and it just wasn't the birth we expected, you know?"

"There's no way to prepare for it."

"Not at all, and then after, no one understands what you've been through." She sat crosslegged on the ground, leaning forward with her hands on her hips, looking angry.

"What happened to Cade was unnecessary. We think labor and delivery messed up."

"Really?"

"They didn't suction her for at least two minutes and they

didn't have any suctioning equipment in the room, and it's possible they should have done a C-section for fetal distress," I said, jumbling it all together.

The woman who sat near us said gently, "It's hard to know sometimes why these things happen. She looks beautiful now."

"Thank you." I smiled. The woman sat on a blanket in the dappled shade, her long pale hair spread over her shoulders. Leo sat placidly on her lap, staring all around with big blue eyes. The other woman looked tight and ugly next to her. Which woman did I look like? The bitter one?

"I'm starting a support group," the bitter one said. "For parents whose babies have been in intensive care. I think it's important to talk."

I told her I wished I could join, but that we were leaving town soon. Fred had just received a fellowship that would take us to Massachusetts for seven months. I resolved not to be angry or bitter. I could accept what had happened to Cade.

One night I lay in bed trying to figure out why I feared the words "cerebral palsy." I disliked the word "cerebral" and had trouble associating it with its meaning, relating to the brain or intellect; to me it sounded base, of the body. And "palsy" summoned up the uncontrolled shaking of the limbs of withered, stunted cripples. Would my baby wither? Would she be set apart from other children, would she walk crookedly down an elementary school hallway, alone and stared at? I had to get over the fear of the label, and understand that cerebral palsy covered many variations in disorder and severity. It didn't spell doom. Even the worst outcome wasn't doom—the idea was frightening, but daily life was not. Parents we knew had children diagnosed with attention-deficit disorder and Tourette's syndrome, and our worries now fell into a similar category, of problems that were not life threatening.

In the Bismarck waiting room, the pediatric neurologist greeted us with, "How did this child get to be so beautiful?" As Dr. Greider ushered us down the hall to his office, he said, "How did she get to be so charming?" A nurse and a woman whom he addressed as Dr. Ming joined us in his office. He sat down in a swivel desk chair. I sat in an armless chair with Cade on my lap, and Fred leaned against an examining table. The nurse and Dr. Ming flanked the closed door.

"What tragic problem has brought you here today?" he asked, smiling. He had a graying light-brown beard like an Amish father; it made a smooth curl over his jawline.

Fred nodded at me. I didn't want to talk, because my voice rasped from a cold, but I'd seen most of the odd movements. "I don't know if it's tragic," I began. "But since April we've noticed odd movements that she makes with her upper body, and—"

"Show Dr. Ming what they look like," Greider said. I put Cade down on the floor. Greider gave her a tennis ball and she took it, saying, "Ba." I demonstrated the undulating movement and the shoulder-hunching, and then the ear-to-shoulder shudder with the curling arm.

He stared down genially at Cade, who offered him the ball. "Is she as smart as she looks?"

"She's learning a new word almost every day."

He directed Dr. Ming to move away from the filing cabinet and he pulled out a long drawer stuffed with papers and rummaged. "Here's what it is." He held up some pages. I took an article entitled "Shuddering Attacks in Children."

"It's a benign condition," he said. "These children get little attacks of shuddering. Sometimes they grow out of them." He swiveled around to Fred. "Hold out your hands," he said. Fred held out his hands and Dr. Greider said, "Yup, very slight tremor. Now you, Mom." I held out my hands and he stood up to examine them. "The fingers jump slightly, see, Dr. Ming?" He held out his own hands. "Mine do that, too. Very common. It's an inherited condition." He sat down in his chair and crossed his legs.

"This has nothing to do with her birth?" I asked.

"Nothing whatsoever. Now what was it that happened to her?"

"She had meconium aspiration syndrome," I said.

"And persistent pulmonary hypertension," Fred said.

He waved his hands. "Nothing to do with that. Just look at her!" Cade was standing up and playing with his shoelace. The nurse smiled down at her. Dr. Ming smiled tiredly, as if she'd been standing up and nodding alertly for too many hours that day.

"Of course she looks great," I said. "But the research we've read indicates that not much is known about the long-term effects of meconium aspiration syndrome."

"What are you reading this stuff for? She's got no problems I can see."

"Since she was delivered so poorly," Fred said. "We felt that as parents, it was our responsibility to do the research."

"Hey, I got no problem with parents educating themselves." Dr. Greider smiled broadly and pointed at the open file drawer. "I hand out articles to parents all day long, I'm giving you articles, but there's no reason to worry about things until they happen. I mean, you can worry about the earthquake, you can fear a car accident—both of which I've been through—or you can just live your life."

"We didn't just decide to be anxious about her—there was good cause to be anxious," I said. "I don't sit in my apartment in the afternoon looking for her to make weird movements."

"If I can't convince you, I can't convince you."

"You diagnosed her five minutes after we walked in here," I said.

"Because I know what the problem is, I've seen it before."

"You have no suspicion of cerebral palsy?" I asked.

"No."

"Even though many cases aren't diagnosed until eighteen months or two years," Fred said.

"Or later," Dr. Greider said. "Sometimes not until adolescence. But the movements you describe are not like cerebral palsy. What, Dr. Ming, are we likely to see in a cerebral palsied child?"

"Hemiparesis," she said quickly.

"Right, or . . ."

"Diparesis." We looked up those terms when we got home; they referred to paralysis of one side of the body, or paralysis primarily of the legs.

"Good. I should charge you folks another five dollars for having Dr. Ming here. The kid's been playing with the tennis ball, she's got great control. No, I'd worry more about her taste in men than any of these problems."

"From what I've read," I said. "A significant proportion of babies with her birth conditions do develop problems, and it takes multiple examinations to determine, so I don't think we're unreasonable to be concerned."

"You know what I think?" He leaned back in his chair. "If they're meant to be good, they're good. If it were my kid, I wouldn't worry."

"The nurse in the Golden Gate program said if it were her kid, she'd want this checked out."

"You have her in Golden Gate? She doesn't need to be in Golden Gate."

"The hospital referred us," Fred said. He was slightly flushed with annoyance; my face felt warm, too. "We didn't take it upon ourselves."

"Golden Gate, Easter Seals. Some people go once and can't stand it. Personally, I think it makes people anxious for no reason.

It would break my heart," he said, "if you were to take your vacation money and spend it on a pediatric neurologist. Some parents will shop the kid around until they find a guy who says there's a problem. It would break my heart to see you spend the money."

When we got to the stairwell, Fred said, "That was awful."

"At least we told him what we thought."

"Not that it made a difference."

We read the article that Dr. Greider had held out as support for his diagnosis, and the description of shuddering attacks in children did not seem altogether relevant to Cade. None of the six children considered for the 1975 study had experienced any birth trauma. But we let ourselves be comforted by the fact that shuddering attacks stopped for these children in the first decade of life.

Cade continued to have tremors, which happened more often when she was hungry, or tired, or ill at ease, and this accorded with the article. I suspected that Cade's colic, her tension, her chronically stuffy nose, and her terror of doctors and their equipment were all related to her birth trauma, though no direct connections could be made. And I believed that the tremors—whether they were tics, attacks, a form of palsy, or a neurological twitch—would not have occurred if she'd had a less traumatic first ten days of life. Surely oxygen deprivation, the ventilator, the morphine, the paralyzing pavulon, the dopamine, or the umbilical catheter had something to do with these movements. No one would say.

The author Thomas Larson has said that people write accounts of traumatic events out of a desire to end the trauma; the self in the present, the survivor, wishes to write about the self in the past, the victim. The one who writes is healed, the one who writes is sealing off the grief of the past.

The desire to end the trauma was like the desire for a perfect birth—one went through a difficult, painful process and then held up the lovely, wriggling, breathing baby and said, I did it! The pregnancy is over, the labor has been suffered, let's take this baby home. Like so many birth stories, ours was messier. I did want to shape it into a history with an end. I did want to seal off the past. Couldn't we proceed without dragging this ugly story behind us? Our friends and relatives didn't want to think about the story anymore. The instant photos of Cade on her warming bed, the respirator tube in her mouth, were mounted in her baby album and it seemed to me that people flicked past them with unexpressed reproach: couldn't we take out those ugly pictures? But we couldn't. Cade's whole life, from beginning to present, lived in her and in us. When she had croup and could hardly breathe, when she hyperventilated at the sight of equipment as harmless as a shoe sizer, her past refused erasure. For me, childbirth would always mean the birth of Cade, with its attendant darkness and mercy.

As time passed, the story's proportions changed. We were still living in the story, but the beginning had receded, and the narrative stretched out farther and farther ahead of us. We'd been large characters in a drama, swallowing hours, occupying rooms. Now we were three tiny figures in a landscape. We walked along the baseball fields in Golden Gate Park. "I've read that children shouldn't have pets until they're six," I said to Fred. "So maybe we'll get her a dog then."

"That's actually good timing because it might die just when she goes to college."

"Perfect."

She leaned sideways out of the stroller and craned around to track a chartreuse tennis ball, a golden retriever jumping after it. We continued our circuit on the path under eucalyptus and pine trees. I was happy, but with a shred of fierceness to protect the moment, interrupt the stream of time.

As Cade grew, the smallest baby clothes seemed like they never could have fit her; we packed them away in boxes. All year Cade replaced herself over and over again, so that the current version seemed like the only possible one. One day it was almost her first birthday.

When I went to bed the night before, I said to Fred, "This was when I was going into labor."

"Oh God," he said, covering his face with a sheet. "Your mother does this. The birth story."

"I am allowed to do it once, mister." I pulled off the sheet. "I was going into labor but I didn't tell you yet."

All the next day I thought about what had been happening exactly a year before. I was grateful to be playing with my baby instead of in labor! At ten o'clock it had been difficult, at noon I had been rocking back and forth in a chair.

"You were getting ready to come out, pookie," I said, poking Cade in the belly. "You were coming to see Mama."

"Mama," she said.

We took her to the zoo in the afternoon, and every once in a while, between pointing out polar bears and giraffes and eating ice cream, I would think, *Now we were at the hospital, now Fred and I were staring at each other, breathing together.* I knew I was playing this little trick on myself whereby I would cheerfully dwell on all the pain of labor, and the relief of delivery and the sight of her looking at me, then stop the story when she was taken away.

My mother's story about the birth of my sister went like this: she went to see Averill Harriman speak, and people in the audience threw tomatoes at him, and she was so angry she didn't realize she was in labor. When she figured it out, my parents rushed to the hospital. My father sat down in a waiting room with the other fathers, who had been sweating in there for hours. He grabbed a magazine, but as soon as he'd opened it a nurse poked her head in and said, "Mr. Rhett?" He looked around the room, as if to say, Me, already? The nurse smiled at him. "You have a baby girl." My mother's story about me, her firstborn, has her water breaking in the middle of the night and my father stumbling around in the dark and dropping car keys. It was a nineteen-hour labor, just like mine. Every year on my birthday, she'll say, "I was sitting in a lawn chair at the edge of a golf course, when I felt the first pains," or "Right about now we were calling the doctor." The story ends with, "And there you were, in my arms."

At 7:24 p.m. on July 28th, exactly one year after Cade's birth, I was nursing her. She was sleepy, having gone without her afternoon nap. Fred was rushing around the neighborhood picking up Thai takeout and a bottle of wine for our dinner after the baby was asleep. We would toast to Cade and to each other, because we'd all passed through, we'd all been transformed. We'd made it this far. Her lungs were supposed to be healed by now. She breathed softly through her nose. Her eyes were closed. She rested a hand on her belly. *You were being born now, honey,* I thought, gazing at the contented baby in my arms. *And here you are.*

The last time I saw Dr. Hanover was for Cade's two-year checkup. He hadn't seen her since she was a month old. Cade hated doctors, nurses, anyone proffering metal instruments. It was once thought that infants didn't feel pain, but new research suggests that not only do they feel pain, but they retain a memory of it that makes subsequent pain more intense. I approached the doctor's appointment braced for the usual screams, with a promise of the toy store afterwards. Cade cried when I undressed her, cried when she was weighed. Then I held her on my lap with a blanket, waiting. When Dr. Hanover came in, he didn't make quacking noises at her, or waggle his fingers in her face, or speak in a ridiculous voice like other pediatricians. He sat calmly in a chair across from us and looked at Cade. She blinked.

"How is she?"

"Just fine." Cade's shudders had stopped by then. Occasionally when she was tense she'd hunch her shoulders, but this movement now appeared to be more of a habit than any actual attack.

He proceeded through the battery of questions about eating, walking, and talking as he checked her ears, eyes, throat, stomach. And she didn't cry, she just stared at him. I had the oddest feeling that she remembered him, his touch or possibly his face, and that the doctor and I knew this but wouldn't say. We are rational people. He hoisted her off the table to check her posture and balance, and she smiled at him.

"She's beautiful."

"Yes."

It seemed that the exam had concluded and he would close his file folder, recap his pen, and leave, but he didn't. He said, "It's hard to believe."

"It is," I said. "If it weren't for you, she wouldn't be here."

I had never thanked him, and it was only over the course of months that the force of my gratitude had grown. He kept oxygen flowing to her brain, I'd think. I hadn't been so conscious of oxygen before, as first, as essential. What could a minute's interruption wreck? Every second, he didn't let her go. And she didn't let go. He wanted us to touch her with our hands; he believed beyond the machines.

He drew with a black felt-tip pen on a tongue depressor, a happy face on one end, a sad face on the other. "Which one is happy," he asked Cade. She took the wooden stick and studied it. I told him I was writing about Cade's birth. He wondered sometimes, he said, what it was like for the parents of babies in intensive care. Would I show him what I'd written when it was done? Of course. He held Cade's hands for a moment. "You are perfect," he said.

Neither of us needed to go to the toy store afterwards. I felt we'd both been given a benediction: You are well.

10

For over two years, almost all of my writing led back to Cade's birth. All roads lead to Rome, I would think tiredly, as I drafted yet another poem which, though perhaps it had begun with imagery of grasslands on the northern California coast, turned out to be about breathing. Where could I go? After we moved to Provincetown, I started running on the fire road near our house during my writing time. On the sand road bordered by pines, I thought I could get out of my mind. I used my eyes to look at ponds crackled with ice, my ears to hear winter birds. Then I'd run into the shack we'd insulated for a study, and write down what I observed. I'm not a good runner. At best I was on a tether to my house, a rubber band that snapped me back when I couldn't breathe anymore in the cold air.

Sometimes Fred would see a small cut or bruise on the back of one of Cade's hands and imagine that it was an IV scar. Sometimes he would contemplate bombing Bismarck Hospital, blowing up the main building in a grand flaming expression of rage and revenge. But he wouldn't. Our baby was a happy, normal toddler. She has no scars. We feel only foolish about our obsessions. The poems I wrote aren't good, only true.

Leonard Kriegel writes in his essay "Wheelchairs," "We don't usually think of liberation as mechanical." The linguistic root of mechanical is "pulley," a contrivance. Cade's liberation was by virtue of machines, the contrivances of electricity, needles, tubes, medications. My liberation was seemingly more natural, though the mind's work of making associations has a certain machine-like quality as it links and joins, pulling one image to another.

Meconium comes from a beautiful word, the Greek mekonion, derived from mekon, or poppy. A current definition of meconium is: the first fecal excretion of a newborn child, composed chiefly of bile, mucus, and epithelial cells. An older definition is, the milky sap of the unripe seed pods of the opium poppy. Don't the two definitions connect in this story? I see dark poppy flowers, the dark meconium stain on my hand, the stunning poison spreading in my baby's lungs, like opium sending her to delirium—then death, if medicine had not saved her.

On a Friday afternoon in June in Provincetown, when Cade was almost three, we planted our first tomatoes. My grandfather grew tomatoes by his front steps at the beach in North Carolina, and I thought that since we lived by the beach now, we'd plant tomatoes, too. We'd never rented a house, or property with a yard before. We were putting the plants in the ground days later than I'd wanted, but it had taken work to clear a rectangular plot in a sunny place next to the steps, and prepare the sandy soil with fertilizer and peat moss. At 5:30, we put six plants in the ground, with green bamboo support stakes, and we watered them together. At just about that time in Washington, D.C., my grandfather, carrying an overnight bag in one hand and a pale blue suit on a hanger in the other, slipped backwards and fell on a brick side-walk. He'd been on his way into a friend's house, ready to attend a party the next day. He hit his head on the bricks, succumbed into coma, and died of cardiac arrest after neurosurgery in the middle of the night.

I'd planned to call him for advice about the tomatoes, but hadn't. Every relative had a regret like that, or worse. My mother had left his bedside after the surgeon assured her he was in fine shape. But then he died, alone. I couldn't sleep that Friday night, and kept thinking how odd it was that we'd put the tomatoes in the ground just as he'd hit his head on the ground, as if there were meaning to be found in that coincidence. I was waiting for the phone to ring, and felt lucky that almost three years had passed since the phone seemed that way in the dark, coiled, electric. The phone rang, of course. Cade and I boarded a plane a few hours later.

Approaching Boston in the twelve-seater Cessna, we could see clustered towns along the shoreline. There were knots of white-trimmed houses, and apartment buildings with back porches stacked like paper trays. Long-legged water towers sat back from the houses, as in our town. So many lives occurred side by side. How could I feel my own so forcibly? Sameness swallowed us all, the same houses, hospitals, cemeteries. The same news. I perceived a simultaneous community and brutality. In the psychiatric hospital, at 17, I'd felt them both. Each of us had an individual story, of swallowing pills or carrying razorblades or driving a tractor (the available vehicle) into a wall. We wore what we wanted, cowboy boots or housedresses or black Led Zeppelin t-shirts, and we acted ourselves—cheerful, nasty, withdrawn—in group therapy. Many of us were relieved to be in a hospital, among fellow patients who understood us. Yet we also felt like raw materials in a factory, being refined to pop out of the front door with discharge papers and a plan for life. When a bell rang, we lined up at the nurse's counter to receive our white paper cup with pills inside. Even my friend who refused meds had to line up for a cup—with vitamins inside. We lined up for breakfast, lunch, and dinner together, pushing plastic trays along the rails. We made bracelets with snap closures, watched television, and kept the doors to our two-bed rooms open. We were diagnosed as x and treated with y.

My friend Kara, who had been living in our household temporarily when I was committed to the hospital, gave me a newspaper article some years ago which described how, in the 1970s, mental health professionals had tended to hospitalize disturbed teenagers rather than treat them as outpatients, at an unprecedented and since unequalled rate. I felt both the sting and relief of being part of a national trend. So my case wasn't special. Just as I wasn't the only girl who read Sylvia Plath in a locked bedroom, with an obsessive empathy. Whatever minor tragedies set me apart also made me a part of something; in fact, in the 1980s, it seemed that a rather high proportion of the graduate students in poetry had experienced forced hospitalization. So our progression is: commitment to the psych ward, earning masters degrees, teaching college composition classes . . .

In Washington, on Saturday afternoon, there were funeral arrangements to be made. After spending hours in Mom's kitchen, where we talked on the phone to relatives and the funeral home, I noticed a large clear plastic bag on one of the wicker armchair stools. Mom was sitting next to it. Inside was Grandpa's stuff: a baby-blue soft polo shirt, white khakis, black nylon socks, white bucks, his teeth. Now I saw the garment bag hanging on the knob of the french door, a small hard suitcase on the floor. I picked up the teeth, stained with blood and food, and said I'd wash them; no, the funeral home would do that. I was grateful. The blue shirt was bloodstained, so Mom threw it out. I took the pants and socks downstairs to wash with a load of household laundry, but before I dropped the pants in the machine I held them to me. I'd never touched Grandpa's clothes before, except when hugging him, though we always took notice of his wardrobe. In summer, he wore the white khakis, which matched his smooth swan-white hair, with a pullover knit shirt, which had to have buttons and a collar. A formal man, he insisted that men wear shirts in the house, even on trips from the deck to the kitchen for a beer. He wore white bucks, even on the beach. I'd never seen him wear sneakers or sandals, never seen his bare feet. I noted the size of his pants, which I've now forgotten, and placed them in the machine, which would wash all of him away.

Between making arrangements and seeing them carried out, Cecily, Fred, and I would go to Philadelphia for my father's heart surgery on Monday morning. The combination of a congenital defect and a recent car accident made mitral valve repair necessary. In the cardiac intensive care unit, aside from the respirator tube entering his mouth, Dad's face didn't look too bad. There was a red swollen bruise on his neck where a line went in. Clear gel on his eyelids and lashes, because anesthesia was dehydrating. His hands were restrained with white ties at the bedrail. "Who's the nurse?" his respiratory therapist asked, as he heard me pointing out the numbers for oxygen concentration, breaths per minute, and pressure. He corrected my definition of voluntary breath. My weak knees surprised me. I sat in a yellow chair. There was the monitor above the bed with heart rate, blood pressure, oxygenation. I explained those, and traced each IV needle to its bag. Nurses kept coming in, rigging bags to metal poles and talking about how well he was doing. We were waiting for the doctor. I felt sick. Dad moved against his restraints; we'd agreed the night before that if he heard us he would move an arm or leg, since he couldn't talk. He struggled to open his sticky eyes. We took turns standing by him, stroking his arm, saying, "It's okay. We're here. You're doing great."

I hated it there, I hated the IV bags, hated waiting for the doctor to come in and pronounce. You never knew when a doctor would come, he'd probably arrive the minute you left to go to the bathroom. There was no reason I had to sit down, except I felt awful. Cecily, whom I'd thought of as squeamish about hospitals, seemed fine. She sat next to me and talked to Leslie, who lived with our father now. I'd thought I would be inured to the hospital, but instead I'd been sensitized. One more intensive care unit might kill me. We had to stay, of course. Our grandfather had just died coming out of anesthesia; we weren't going anywhere until our dad was safe. The doctor came in. Leslie's son Ethan is a movie actor. The doctor said to him, "Please, my daughter loves you, she'd be so happy for your autograph." They'd had to go into our father's heart twice, the doctor said, because the first repair was inadequate. He'd been brought almost back to consciousness, then reanesthetized, so he'd take a while to wake up. "What was that movie you were in this spring?" the doctor asked. There was a red monitor light taped to Dad's left index finger, and we couldn't touch that hand. Just like Cade. This room took me back to where I didn't want to be. In the intensive care nursery, I'd been stunned by exhaustion and surprise, but now I was fully aware of how frightening it had felt.

He started to wake, and only two of us could be in the room at once then. What a relief it was to leave and go sit in the waiting room until my turn. Dad was thirsty. He mouthed "wat" around the respirator tube, pantomimed pouring water from a pitcher with his restrained hand. "Water?" we said, and he nodded vigorously. But he couldn't have water, not until the respirator tube had been out for six hours. Maybe it had been easier to watch a baby's unarticulated suffering. Maybe pavulon had been a blessing for us; we didn't have to witness Cade's pain, since she had appeared to sleeping. He was partially awake when we left late at night.

Our grandfather's funeral was a new machine. His body was laid out in a flag-draped open coffin for the family to see, in a small room off of a larger grieving parlor. We could sit and cry on the green couches or wander over to look at his set face, mouth in a straight line. All his beautiful hair had been shaved for surgery, and the only hat we had was a fishing cap. Its bill stuck up over the coffin edge. His spirit was gone, anyone could see that. He was just a body, and it was criminal to look, and retain that image of him. Only his hands appeared like him, gnarled and purpled from work. At 86, he'd still climbed ladders to nail up shingles, fix storm windows. He gardened, raised the flag, barbecued, drove his two-toned green Cadillac. Of course the funeral directors felt oily, of course they accepted our baggie of his garden roses and promised to put them in the coffin.

The church didn't like us. We wanted someone to sing "Joe Hill" because Grandpa was a union organizer in the 1930s, but that wasn't a religious song. They wouldn't allow it. I'd formatted the program slightly wrong, misplacing the psalm selection, and the minister corrected me as soon as I walked in. I didn't know my bible. We'd chosen Tennyson's "Crossing the Bar" to be read, which we felt reflected Grandpa's life by the sea and his uncertainty about God. The five of us grandchildren had written up memories of our grandfather, read by a friend, in which we described how Grandpa had made a haven for us of rituals and manners. We were five grandchildren whose parents divorced, and through the years we could all count on being asked to peel shrimp and hammer down the deck boards, hose every grain of sand off our feet before venturing into the carpeted house, and have a slice of the chocolate cake he'd baked. There was a part in there about his solicitude for dogs, and we even speculated that maybe our beloved dog Teddy was up in heaven with Grandpa right now, cooking enchiladas. I think the minister, who sat still in her white robes, almost choked there. We all sobbed on cue, walking down the aisle behind his coffin. The ritualized burial at Arlington felt like a gift, with its choreographed twenty-one gun salute and prayers. We sat in folding chairs with bowed heads, and then we stood, and then we placed roses and sand on the coffin. Miles of stones shone in the sun, with carved names, ranks, and two dates. That was all, pure summaries.

Fred had to return to work the next day, and so after the funeral reception we drove back to Provinceton, spontaneously detouring to Philadelphia to visit my dad. He had a fever, so my anxiety felt warranted. Cade skipped around the hospital room, not bothered by the staples in his chest. We stayed for an hour, talking with Leslie and his nurse, then drove towards home. At three a.m., Fred fell asleep at the wheel. Fred and I woke when we hit the center guard rail, and Cade woke when we stopped just short of hitting the side embankment.

"It's okay," Fred said.

"No, no," I moaned at him. "No, it's not okay."

I was shivering. We were all still buckled in, and Cade's carseat hadn't moved. I can't remember if she spoke or cried, just that she was awake, and we held her hands. We asked her to move her head and she could. The headlights shone on the grassy yellow-green embankment, a vertical wall we hadn't hit. We were on the divided highway that runs from Providence to the Cape, untrafficked at this hour.

"What happened?" I said.

Fred opened his door, which gave a resisting whine. He examined a long horizontal crease in the metal. "We hit the guard-rail," he said, looking across the road at it. "I turned right and tried to stop the car."

"We could have hit the embankment," I said.

Every time we traveled this highway after, we searched for the guardrail we'd hit, but couldn't identify it; we only knew we were lucky to have hit it, because there were stretches without rails, there were bridges over water, and there were thousands of pine trees. I'd only been asleep for ten minutes. I didn't have a driver's license, having let mine expire years before because of a fear of driving. So Fred had to do all the driving. My job was to navigate, dispense food, entertain Cade, and keep him awake. In high school, a friend fell asleep at the wheel and almost died after hitting a tree. His fellow passenger, also asleep at the time, was thrown clear. After that, I swore I'd never be in a car where the driver was the only one awake. I'd keep the driver company. And I always had. But this one night, I was so tired. And Fred had told me to sleep. And ten minutes later, he had fallen asleep. While chewing gum, to his surprise. We should have stopped at a motel in Connecticut, but somehow in the stress of the funeral and the surgery, we'd concluded that Fred absolutely had missed enough work and had better be back in the office by morning. He climbed back in the car. We were at home by five o'clock. The air smelled like a campground after our days in the cities. We were safe. Our families hadn't gotten terrible phone calls in the middle of the night. The intensity of the bundled events left me tired, my body aching, but my mind awoke to a slow clarity: *we were alive.* We might just as easily have been dead.

Fred and I had been in one other car incident together, when we'd done a 360 on an icy Wisconsin road at night. We were traveling sixty miles an hour when we hit black ice and turned, slowly it seemed, watching snowfields spin by panoramically. "We're okay," he kept saying, and I said it, too. We didn't hit anything. We were pointing in the right direction when we stopped. When we arrived at our friends' house in Madison, we asked for scotch. A week later, we decided to get married, and so I wonder now if our moments of joint terror jolt us forward, because soon after hitting the guardrail we decided to have a second child.

There had been months when I couldn't imagine experiencing labor and delivery again. With a visceral fear, I felt that maybe I couldn't give birth right, and the next baby might even die. We had been so lucky with Cade, who was healthy, sweet-natured, and smart. People exclaimed over her in supermarkets, libraries, restaurants. Look at those curls! I've never seen a little one behave so well! While curls and obedience didn't matter so much to me, I privately agreed she was extraordinary. So why push our luck? Another child could never be like this one. *But of course not,* I thought; *another child would be a whole new individual.* I was curious about who this new person might be. And I'd grown up with a sibling—I couldn't imagine being without Cecily. Cade would like a sibling, too. Two parents and two children seemed like a good balance of relationships. I suppose it simply felt normal to me.

Over the preceding year, it had taken me a long while to understand why Fred might not want another child. I assumed that having come from a family of five children, more than one child would feel normal to him, too. But I think he felt that to be an only child would be a privilege; being one of many children meant that when your father got fired from his job, you had to wait in line for food stamps and drink powdered milk and not play hockey because the equipment was expensive. Pragmatically, he didn't want a second child for the same reasons he hadn't wanted a first child: we'd be poorer, more tired, less romantic with each other, more homebound, and less able to write. He was correct, of course. So I collected magazine articles about the benefits of only children, for both children and parents. I considered various theories about why I wanted a second child: I was blindly repeating the pattern of my childhood instead of considering what was right for me; I was a conventional twentieth century American; I was biologically driven to reproduce; I was afraid of devoting myself to writing and failing, which childbearing would prevent; I'd already given up on being ambitious as a writer, and mothering gave me something to do. All of these were weighed and turned around for their elements of truth. Ultimately, though, I couldn't think my way out of the desire.

Our whole unpleasant year-long discussion was strangely positive, because we both realized that our decision about a second child had nothing to do with what had happened to Cade. Her ordeal intensified certain feelings and made us irrational—for Fred, we wouldn't just be tired with a second child, we'd be flattened with exhaustion. For me, labor wasn't just nervewracking, it was terrifying. But now I knew I wanted two children, and only needed to transcend my fear. I felt calm and maternal and determined and right.

By the end of August, our second baby was conceived. Later I'd lie in bed feeling stunned that I was pregnant. It was lonely. Over the year my pregnancy occasionally felt like another of our projects or jobs: Fred was teaching three classes, developing a graduate writing program, and editing an anthology of postmodern American fiction; I was teaching one class, editing an anthology of memoirs, and growing a baby. Reading pregnancy books, following the right diet, scheduling obstetrician appointments, and ministering to my various discomforts were all responsibilities of my employment.

In November a first, nearly invisible snow fell, and I felt the baby move while I lay in bed looking out the windows. Tiny, intermittent pulses like the snow floating in the air. I was only fifteen weeks pregnant. Later an ultrasound technician would tell us it was a boy, and we would name him Jacob Rhett Leebron. I am happy to know he's a boy and name him, because he feels real to me. He's already a person—all he needs to do is survive the birth passage. We live as if he will live, unpacking baby clothes, bidding on a house with a room for a nursery. All of the grandparents have volunteered to come help with the baby, and I have welcomed them this time, knowing how much I need them. So we pencil in weeks on the calendar, as if an actual baby will be here, nursing and crying and spitting up. I can hardly believe it. Cade carries around a doll named Jacob, her baby brother, and she wants him to have formula instead of breastmilk so that he can sleep in her room and she can feed him bottles at night.

I am afraid he'll die. We took a tour of the Carolinas Medical Center in the town where we live now, Charlotte. The maternity center is luxurious, with a well-baby nursery, private rooms for new mothers, and labor rooms equipped with showers, rocking chairs, and cable television. One mother on the tour was very concerned about bonding, with making sure the nurses didn't whisk her baby away to be weighed and measured. She wanted the baby placed in her arms first, and left there for as long as possible. Meanwhile Fred and I examined the banks of medical equipment cleverly concealed behind panels. Yes, each room had infant resuscitation equipment. No, residents didn't work in this center; they worked in the clinic maternity center on another floor, where women without health insurance gave birth. Each woman on this floor had her own labor and delivery nurse, and a licensed physician for delivery. And, the tour guide announced proudly, CMC was the only hospital in the region with an ECMO, a heart-lung machine. Fred and I shared a look: this is the hospital for us. Forget bonding—we want the heart-lung machine.

I work on imagining that I'll go through labor and push out the baby, and the nurses will clean him up, and he'll be handed to me, and then I'll move to a maternity room, and he'll be brought there, and Fred will bring champagne, and we'll use the telephone to call our families with the good news, and Cade will come sit on the bed and meet her brother. That's as far as I get. What if I have to tell her that her baby brother died?

The poor child. School was cancelled for an ice storm the day we met our new obstetrician, and so she accompanied us to the appointment. He asked about my last labor and birth, and I told him, feeling like a hysteric. I almost begged him to tell me it wouldn't happen again, or that at least if there were meconium he'd order an emergency cesarean.

"It's case by case," he said sensibly. "Sometimes we see meconium in the amniotic fluid, but it's only a slight green stain, and we proceed with a normal delivery."

"But that will really upset me," I said, "if you see meconium, I won't think it's okay."

He shrugged. Cesareans aren't performed on demand.

Since that appointment, Cade will pick up a doll and tote it along, telling a story like, "This is my baby brother. He had meconium so he had to stay in the hospital, but now he's home and he can't breathe so we have to let him rest." I wonder what her teachers think. If something happens to Jacob, I know she'll transmute it into story, as she has with the deaths of dogs and cats she's known, and the death of her great-grandfather. Though I've told her in my academic way that no one can know if there's a heaven, she seized onto the concept immediately. Sometimes we pretend we're in heaven with all the dead we know, and we're having a picnic on a blanket. Even if they can't live down here with us, we can visit by pretending, and we can resurrect them just as surely as we pass sandwiches made of the parts of toys. Because a story is the passage through grief, to possibility.

We are swimming, Cade and I. She is almost four. I am eight months pregnant and we lie in Atlantic-blue sheets in the double bed, waking and sleeping. Her arms are around my neck, we lie on our sides, my enormous belly between us. I have to teach a class tonight, and am exhausted, having been up with her for two hours in the middle of the night. Fred is at school, teaching his graduate seminar. I can't sleep, but am floating, or cutting through shallow waves like a ship's prow. Cade was my grandfather's middle name, and I was disheartened to learn one of its definitions: abandoned, as in a cade lamb left by its mother, raised by humans. *We abandoned our baby to machines,* I'd often thought as I held her to me fiercely, *but we're together now.* We've moved too many times, to Massachusetts, back to California, to Massachusetts again, then here to North Carolina. My grandfather owned a house by the ocean in North Carolina for thirty years. Thirty years he walked the wooden deck, raised and lowered the flag. Now I live nearby but he is dead. Older gentlemen with waved white hair speak of barbecue, glide by in Cadillacs, drawl matter-of-factly, but they are not him. The people in the apartment complex where we live come from Sweden, from Russia, from New Jersey. We all have taupe carpeting that squeaks when you walk on it. Our bed squeaks but we can't find the source. At night I turn and turn again, my ribs aching, and the bed squeaks, and I could be a ship heaving from side to side. Now Jacob moves his fists and heels in arcs across me. It is night for him, and it is the ocean, all our sounds distorted. He must live. When I have a lot of contractions, usually in the evening, I lie down. I float and imagine lying in water, or being in the greenest place, sheltered by damp grass and blooming hedges. There are flame-flickers of panic at the edges of my pictures. Fred and I watch the childbirth preparation videotape every few days to practice breathing, relaxing muscles. *It doesn't matter,* I think, *what you pack in the hospital bag or how you breathe.* Some women have thirteen children. Is anything under their control? When I sleep I dream of manuscripts I'm editing, papers I'm grading, mortgage applications, all white papers with gray type, gray scrawled lettering I can't read. These sheets have a paisley pattern, which makes as much sense as language, pale amoeba swimming on an inky sea. This afternoon I see myself and Cade in the ceiling light fixture, a piece of moon-glass. Our breaths are invisible rivers. I see her long blondish curls against her navy blue dress, her hazel eyes opening and closing. Her lashes, two crescents.